SOUTHERN PIONEERS

SOUTHERN PIONEERS
IN SOCIAL INTERPRETATION

EDITED BY

HOWARD W. ODUM

*Kenan Professor of Sociology and Director of the
School of Public Welfare, University
of North Carolina*

Essay Index Reprint Series

Originally published by:
THE UNIVERSITY OF NORTH CAROLINA PRESS

BOOKS FOR LIBRARIES PRESS, INC.
FREEPORT, NEW YORK

First published 1925
Reprinted 1967

PRINTED IN THE UNITED STATES OF AMERICA

PREFACE

The characterization of a leader who "worked while we his fellows lived" and during "such times as are forever running across the loom of human destiny" is a fair one for the first Southern Pioneer of this volume. To a lesser degree perhaps, but nevertheless with fairly specific application, we may think of Mr. White's apt phrases in connection with the other sketches—Aycock, Page, Knapp, Longstreet, Harris, Washington, Breckinridge, Graham. Of these leaders whose contributions have resulted from hard work and devotion to special causes rather than to any dominance of self, the South cannot know too much. They were leaders who looked forward, whose personalities and capacities they were willing and able to adapt to changing needs and whose messages seem almost startlingly timely now.

One of the outstanding features of recent literature has been the wealth of biographical material and the enthusiasm with which our American folk are turning to the study of strong personalities. There are yet other personalities of charm and force whose ideals have not yet found full expression. The brief stories presented in this volume, most of which have been published in *The Journal of Social Forces,* are offered in the belief that the South can ill afford, especially at this time of "growing pains," to forget these leaders and their work. This book is a companion volume to a previous one "Robert E. Lee: An Interpretation," by Woodrow Wilson, and it is hoped that the demand for studies of southern leadership will be such as to justify other volumes in the series.

H. W. O.

CHAPEL HILL, N. C.
March, 1925.

CONTENTS

		PAGE
I.	INTRODUCTORY: A Southern Promise.... *Howard W. Odum*	1
II.	Woodrow Wilson .... *Gerald W. Johnson*	29
III.	Walter Hines Page .... *Robert D. W. Connor*	51
IV.	Charles Brantley Aycock .... *Edwin A. Alderman*	69
V.	Seaman A. Knapp .... *Jackson Davis*	87
VI.	Augustus Baldwin Longstreet .... *John Donald Wade*	117
VII.	Joel Chandler Harris .... *Julia Collier Harris*	141
VIII.	Booker T. Washington .... *Monroe N. Work*	165
IX.	Madeline McDowell Breckinridge ...... *S. P. Breckinridge*	183
X.	Edward Kidder Graham .... *Robert D. W. Connor*	203

SOUTHERN PIONEERS

INTRODUCTORY

A Southern Promise

BY

HOWARD W. ODUM

A SOUTHERN PROMISE

Leaders of the first order in the Nation have come out of the South. The South has now much of the same admixture of blood and social heritage that produced George Washington, Thomas Jefferson, Robert E. Lee, Andrew Jackson, Woodrow Wilson, Walter Hines Page, and other men of distinction. Moreover, the South has an excellent physical environment for the development of strong personalities. Why, then, are the Southern States so barren of individual leaders who represent the highest achievement in their fields? In politics, in education, in literature, in art, in industry, in religion, in any aspect of human endeavor, where are there to be found in the South leaders occupying the foremost place in their respective groups? Or how many even are there who have attained more than mediocre rank?

I

At the outset, however, let it be remembered that the shortage of leadership is being lamented generally throughout the states and elsewhere. One need only call the roll of the great and near-great in the national political parties or in congress or in the realm of international community.

If one feels inclined to complain that certain of
the Southern States are "the worst led states"
in the Union, he may also catalogue the strife
and bickerings or reactionary inertia of other
states. If he grieves over the fact that there are
almost twice as many persons of distinction
born in a certain Southern State as now reside
within its borders, he need only look for comparison to certain other states, Ohio, Indiana,
Iowa, Pennsylvania, Maine, New Hampshire,
even Wisconsin, for similar conditions. Other
states there are whose roll of distinction is not
long. No, the South is not alone in its present
dearth of distinctive leadership if it be compared
with individual states in other regional divisions
of the Union.

There is another point of emphasis which the
South shares with the rest of the country, and
with much of the rest of the world. It is the
changing basis upon which leadership is now
developed and made effective. There are many
aspects of this transfer of emphasis, and many
grounds, therefore, for crudeness and poverty
in the transitional stages. Of course it has long
since been recognized that leadership has been
transferred from kings to people and that we no
longer educate for royalty. But what has become of the leader with "authority," whether in
government, in church, in industry or elsewhere
in which the bigness of the leader is measured

by the subjection of his followers? What has become of the dominant leadership of the church? Is there being transferred from capital to labor much of the important leadership of the future? Has there been a transfer of leadership from country life and agricultural groups to city and industrial folk? Is the dominance of lawyer and politician being taken over by farmer and worker? Has the one-man super-domination epoch given way to the crowd, and if so how much mob and how much democracy? Has the family surrendered its leadership to other agencies? What will be the effect of woman's enlarging leadership? Is the leadership of youth encroaching upon that of maturity? Is Mr. Babbitt taking the place of the former man of professional distinction?

Whatever changes there are, the leaders of the future will approximate an antithesis of the old leaders of the political, military, or religious type. They will be leaders who represent movements and their leadership will draw its strength from the cause represented rather than from the overpowering individual. Alexander and Napoleon, indicted on many counts and sentenced to much labor, would scarcely be respectable in the modern community. So would the great men of yesterday be shorn of their glory by the social codes of today. However perfected in type and technique the old leaders were, the world will know them no more forever. In their stead will be a diffused leadership, of the untapped potential resources of which the world yet knows little. The task of developing this leadership is the task of the present. The verdict of the future may well agree with Joseph K. Hart that "a democracy cannot survive unless all the people, or the greater part of them, possess the quality of potential leadership and the actual leaders possess a deep sense of social responsibility and quality of potential loyalty to other leaders." Many of our deficiencies in present-day leadership are due to the failure so far to make quick adjustments to social change and to the shortness of time for the evolution of new types. The South is far from being an exception to the rule.

II

If this failure to make adjustments to social and economic change in the aspects of transfer of leadership already mentioned be charged against the Southern States in general, as a first count, the second deficiency may be said to grow out of the first. It is that the South lacks experience and training for the newer leadership. By this I do not mean merely the normal deficiencies of after-war desolation, real and tragic as they have been. I mean rather the specific situation in which the leaders of the present

South have had neither experience nor training for leadership outside the atmosphere of political strife, economic limitations, educational and social deficiencies, and general mediocrity in many aspects of life. How, then, could they lead with distinction or govern well? Or how attain an equal place in the last half century of rapid development? Who were the old Southern leaders, the lawyers, the mayors, the judges, the statesmen? Consider today the same communities, towns, cities, states in which they held forth; how many of their children now occupy the same positions of leadership as did their fathers? If their children have not come into the succession others have. Who are they but the chance representatives of the diffused leadership previously referred to, but whose potential abilities have in no wise been brought out or tested? Some there are of the same heritage as the old leaders; more there are of the common folk, mixed here and there and everywhere in a varied composite of the land. Now whatever else may be said of the old Southern leaders; whatever their shortcomings in democratic standards, in attitudes toward the negro and the working man, there can be no doubt that they stood forth in their leadership as examples of distinction, charm, order, force, character. They led. And while the younger leaders, of mottled mien, do have many ideas in advance of their predecessors, and may have in them the making of another generation of distinction, they do not stand out as did the leaders of the Old South. This does not mean that the present status is a final criterion any more than the first efforts of women in politics will prove to be the permanent mode or index of ability. It means simply that here is a new generation with limited experience, limited training and limited leisure but with the abundance of energy, enthusiasm, and small-town adolescent zest for participating in politico-social activities and for enacting righteousness.

As a rule too much significance is attached to temporary results that come from lack of experience and education. There is a vast amount of difference between judgments based upon limited experience and education and those arising from low intelligence or potential intelligence for future generations. Witness the foolish things which any previous generation of folk have done. The distinguished father of a future leading progressive thanks the Lord for the lowly fly, mankind's faithful scavenger! The parents of a leader in hygiene education are mortally afraid of night air! The embittered Virginian in his last will and testament bequeaths to his children and grandchildren and their descendants "throughout all generations, that bitter hatred and everlasting malignity of my heart and soul against the Yankees, including all the people north of the

Mason and Dixon's line—to instill in the hearts of their children and grandchildren, and all future descendants, from childhood, this bitter hatred and those malignant feelings against the aforesaid people and their descendants throughout all future time and generations." If nearly all of his children marry above the Mason and Dixon's line and become generous lovers of a generous people, is it therefore a matter of intelligence or mellowed time and experience? Is progress of scientific son over enthusiastic father a matter of more intelligence, or is dogmatic limitation of father a permanent handicap to the distinguished son to be? Or what man of distinction does not blush to think of youthful statements made, or early convictions for which he has proclaimed himself willing to make the great sacrifice, or make a fool of himself generally? Is he now, in the glow of his prestige and honor, the more intelligent or merely more learned and experienced? If one be inclined to consider these merely academic questions, unrelated to his severe judgments upon the folk, let him inquire into the history of peoples and let him look forward to the future of the governing groups in the grand old empire of Britain, in the coming government of women, and in the newer aspirations of race and common man. The measure of experience today ought not to be the fruit of tomorrow.

Finally, this poverty of the South in experience and training is not found alone in the field of politics and general leadership. "Blessed are the poor in spirit," but the Southern people have not been poor in spirit. Rather they have been poor in almost every other way. And theirs has not been the kingdom of achievement or leadership or Heaven or anything else save perhaps the kingdom of the proud spirit and the glory that was old! In education, in wealth, in public health and public welfare, in the development of the people and homes and farms of the countryside, in literature, in art and in many other fine things we lack the opportunity and experience for leadership and distinction. Even in religion and morality, for which we claim so much, we have been poor in the fruits of social righteousness, justice, and the essence of Christianity. The religion that boasts much, complains continuously, seeks motes in other people's eyes, klans together for persecution, mobs the weak, has little respect for truth, is selfishly self-centered, is emotionally and lazily inclined toward the easiest way, would hardly be expected to produce distinguished creative contributions in any field. So long as the majority of leaders and the great group of followers are rich in that spirit of self righteousness, of sensitive antagonism toward things not our own or of our way of thinking, so long will the South be thrice not blessed.

III

The third count against us is that we have lacked universities. "Tommy" Wilson at home becomes Woodrow Wilson at Princeton. The mediocre lawyer at Atlanta, from Southern fields becomes Woodrow Wilson, the political scientist, teacher, university president, governor, President of the United States from Johns Hopkins. Walter Hines Page, restless youth, hunting for himself, critical of his surroundings, from Johns Hopkins finds the promise of a great leader. Scores of men today in places of distinction began their careers of achievement, ambition, redirected purpose from the larger universities of this country, many of them remained permanently away from the South. Other scores, of the same blood and heritage and potential ability, but without this opportunity, have never developed. Count the men from the South—there are hundreds—who have achieved distinction, whether inside or outside, and see how many have had their pushing force from the outside. In fact we measure our professional folk by the extent to which they hold degrees from Northern and Western universities, albeit often complaining of the bad influence of those universities upon us. What right have we, in all fairness and justice to the South, to pass judgment upon Southern capacity to produce distinction when, by our own and by all estimates, we withhold the means and stimulus for distinguished effort and service?

Perhaps the worst part of the situation is the fact that the great majority of our Southern group, including many colleges and universities, do not think in terms of university. And by this I do not mean merely the physical plant or the student body which goes to make a university, but the spirit of the university, such as that implied in President Chase's recently stated obligation of giving the student a chance to find and love the truth. We have had in the South a few examples of campaigns being made to build great universities, but too often when anything approaching university standards is suggested a halt is called. Much of the propaganda for finance is too often based on the demagogic appeal to religious or local stubbornness or pride, all of which instead of giving us the universities for which we set out, will delay that much longer the coming of real universities. Consider, for instance, a Southern denominational leader proclaiming in his campaign for financial support for "the South's greatest University" that the South "must endow and equip its own institutions of learning, and then by the most watchful care keep them clear of liberalism and liberalists. This is a high and holy obligation which the South owes the great Republic of which it is so important a part." Contrast this then with the estimate of that other Southerner, former president of Princeton and at the time of this utterance at the University of Paris, President of the United States. "University spirit," he said, "is intolerant of all things that put the human mind under restraint. It is intolerant of everything that seeks to retard the advancement of ideals, the acceptance of truth, the purification of life." Contrast it also with the dream of President G. Stanley Hall of universities of the future as the shrine and power house of the research spirit that shall permeate the whole field of inquiry into human knowledge and human welfare. His "University Invisible" would be "composed of all those everywhere who are smitten with the passion of adding something to the sum of the world's knowledge."

Not all of our limitations in college and university are due to ignorance of university standards or lack of university experience and training. Lack of resources, the poverty of material things already referred to, of course is responsible for much. I have before me now an earnest request from one of the more progressive smaller institutions for women asking for a teacher whose classes will include family case work, child welfare, community organization, social pathology, labor problems, economic theory, economic history, and of course some social theory. And the head of the department, holding his doctorate

from one of the largest universities of the land,
ought to know better. Other illustrations are
legion. Thus much of the teaching and claims
of the smaller institutions become superficial.
Many of the smaller institutions in both state
and church are clearly hypocritical in claiming
what they manifestly do not have. This claim
and this atmosphere, as well as the limitations
themselves, tend to lower standards and certainly do not provide the educational leadership
needed. There are other defects that hold back
even the best of beginnings. One of these is the
prevailing tendency for trustees of colleges and
universities, in both state and denominational
schools, to assume both the legislative and
administrative functions of the institution, med-
dling with minute details of internal administration, and limiting faculty, administration and
even students in their normal performance of
duty. There are, of course, notable exceptions
to such a general state, both among the smaller
schools and the larger ones. And the fact that a
Southern university has recently been admitted
into membership of the Association of American
Universities, and is now president of this body,
is evidence both of the exception and also of the
South's ability to develop and maintain universities. It is also evidence that in the past the
South has not had such universities, there being
only one other Southern university member of

this group—a charter member from the beginning.

IV

The South has lacked an atmosphere conducive to achievement and distinction. We have already said that the South has an excellent physical environment for the development of strong personalities. There are fewer more absurd assumptions than that which attributes the South's lack of achievement to climate or southern physical conditions of soil, topography, or other geographical and physical conditions. On the contrary, it will be shown in time that the South's charm of climate, variety of situations, richness of physical setting, coupled with newer social and educational attainments, will prove a superior land for the nurture of leaders and for the promotion of the finer things of life. What we mean in this statement is that there has been no suitable social, cultural, and spiritual atmosphere in which leadership could develop or distinction survive. Besides the limitations of experience and universities already referred to there has been conflict between races, between classes, between denominations, between visible and invisible government, between dominant demagogues and their following. With conflict has come protest. For years now the dominant note has been negative and the South has been sensitive and "against" the things that are progressive and the things that are not her own. And within her borders she has built up faction and clique, the one against the other, all against outsiders. One can scarcely believe that this querulous pessimistic South is the same South of the heroic fighters of the war between the states, or the earlier cheerful optimists, or that of the epic struggle to rebuild her devastated estate. Furthermore, the South is afraid, not of negro domination, but of itself, of each other, afraid to speak the truth or act justly because of what the folks will say; and as Gerald Johnson says, afraid of its eighty million northern critics. A South so depressing in atmosphere cannot achieve; and to remain so, in the face of all her natural resources and her ethnic and social inheritance, would prove one of the most abortive epochs in recent history.

There are, however, heavy tasks ahead if this cumulative atmosphere is to be changed before it alters the whole structure of the South. We have pointed out before the fact that we are ignorant. How could we be otherwise in the face of past experience? But even so, with the handicap of poverty and struggle now happily past, we are not learning enough of the great truths of science or attaining knowledge of social facts and social righteousness. We are afraid of the truth and have few leaders to guide us in its paths. We have pointed out before how little we read and how we fall short of the rest of the country and of our reasonable expectations. And much of the limited reading is of the inbred sort of provincial passing type. We have pointed out the fact that we rank low in creative effort, in writing worthwhile literature, and that we are not willing to pay the price for an achievement which many reliable critics believe lies within the grasp of Southern talent. And in other fields, in the beautifying of our country homes and farms, in the planning of towns, in the building of school houses, and in many other aspects of material achievement the South has come to reflect itself in terms of second rate standards and as not willing to sink individual opinion and financial cost into the common good.

In its sensitiveness the South is still hot-headed, emotional, unthinking in its attitude toward many questions and toward those who do not agree with its opinions or traditions, or those who do not approve of its conduct. This is especially true of matters relating to race, religion, industry, and outside criticism. On the other hand, the South is boastful and superficial with reference to its achievements. Of course it has so long been considered backward that its defence mechanisms would naturally develop something of this sort; and of course the statements made about it have often been hard to bear. Further, it would seem to deserve recognition for what it is achieving, for like Lincoln's ginger bread, no one ever liked it more or had less of it. Nevertheless, it is in grave danger, as has been proved in certain sections, of crippling its future achievement through the constant backward look or the prideful boast of mediocrities. Blessed are the meek, but the South has not been meek nor has it thereby inherited much of the earth. The South is too proud of its non-progressive fundamentalism and enjoys an easy-going rationalism which places entirely too much responsibility for its shortcomings upon the Lord. The South, claiming to be preeminently Christian, is yet in many instances in danger of breeding a gross spirit of boastful materialism with ecclesiastical dogmatism and of joining political demagoguery in unholy alliance with religious fervor, thus producing a mongrel barrenness, the despair of classification. Such an atmosphere coupled with ignorance and intolerance will scarcely produce leaders of distinction.

The South has not accorded due recognition to merit within its own borders. By this I do not mean merely the "prophet without honor" habit, which after all is one of the social order's best mechanisms for the development of its fledgelings. Nor do I mean simply that recurrence of the South's failure to recognize such men as Walter Hines Page or Woodrow Wilson; for, as Professor Connor points out, much of this was their own fault. Nor even do I mean only the failure of the South ever to recognize or follow them except to further its own plans or to please its vanity. It need not be replied that the South takes great pride in its distinguished sons who, having departed from its midst, return to receive acclaim. The South has not yet shown that this enthusiasm is more than a glorification of southern achievement. We mean more than all these; we mean a recognition that includes position, financial reward, esteem and an atmosphere for work, and the privilege of free speech and unhampered proper personal pursuit of achievement.

The factor of inadequate financial support is an element of the situation, not a censure of past performance. But as a fact it is a most powerful and determining element and one which must be reckoned with in the future. And the future is what counts. It is but natural that in the past a region characterized by the limitations already mentioned, should not only be unable to meet the financial terms of more prosperous and experienced sections, but also that it should develop an atmosphere unfriendly to larger rewards. There is, however, less reason for a critical and jealous state of mind on the part of professional or common folk which tends to discourage adequate salaries or suitable pay for professional work. In particular, there is no excuse for the attitude of many of the approximating richer folk which holds, to all intents and purposes, that teachers, professors in colleges and universities, or literary folk, ought to be thankful for whatever salaries or financial rewards may be apportioned to them by their generous boards. They are in it simply for the money anyway and should be employed if they are of the faith and can be had cheap enough. Such an attitude adds immensely to the attractiveness of better positions and higher salaries in other places. It is, of course, often the lack of appreciation as measured by small salaries, rather than the limited salaries themselves, which constitutes the turning point.

If to the absence of a sympathetic atmosphere or of appreciation of progressive social, economic or political effort, or of creative work, be added denial of freedom of speech or opportunity to produce, how much surplus energy, ability or power must one put forth to achieve even an average? And of that average what chance is there for objective measurement or visible recognition? This, again, is no mere academic question, for there are many who make no pretense of speaking or writing freely. Then there is that great number who, surrendering little by little, gradually benumbed through easy-going

rationalization from the promise of great things
to static acquiescence, who do not know that
they do not know. How many manuscripts
there are unpublished, how many positive impulses unobeyed, or how many progressive
steps there remain untaken because of the surety
of vanishing position and influence, no one of
course knows. But I do know of many. Nor is
the prevailing forbidden fruit limited to radical
doctrines in politics, economics, education, religion or sociology, but restrictions encompass
the simple, sincere, courageous telling of the
truth about the South, its people, its history, its
tasks. Indeed, the atmosphere of fear is not
limited to Herrin, or to the common folk of the
South. It permeates the whole body politic.

And of what sort is the merit which we do
recognize within and without the South? There
could be named, of the older group still living,
five score individuals now in the South whose
abilities, personalities and achievements, in a
fair field of opportunity and support, would
easily rank among the first order in any larger
company. And of the younger group I should
gladly undertake to find another outstanding
one hundred with promise as great or greater
than these. Of course they are held in high
esteem in the home state in smaller ways, but
who follows them? What recognition do they
have? What time, means, opportunity and irre-

sistible impulses have they had since the first days of their promise? Who outside of local groups ever knows of their abilities or benefits from their work? Or what larger promise have they for the future? Who are they, on the other hand, by whose reputations the South is known and whose leadership the South follows and esteems? Are they not far too frequently the demagogues and the dogmatists in politics and religion?

And here is a peculiar thing, a sort of *para-doxum paradoxorum*. With all of our agitated protest against outside suggestion or inter-ference and all our enacted "home boy" and "home talent" appointments to the great major-ity of positions, nevertheless when we have dis-tinction or honor to confer, advice to publish, money to pay for services, forthwith we hasten to find someone from afar off upon whom to bestow honor, in return for which we expect kind words, high praise, and local commendation for having brought the great of earth to our small town. Indeed the chief service rendered by our distinguished visitors is usually our own verdict that we have got the best of talent for fortuitous display. If there be home folks with-in the domain of the Southern States let them consider it high honor to pay their own expenses and attend conferences, universities, but let them not presume to know more than the local folks or expect financial reward or appreciation. If there be those from afar, let them know forsooth that we have the willingness and ability to pay whatever is necessary, and the more the honorarium the more we neglect the rest of the program. It is commonly assumed in the South that nothing which might be produced there can possibly be of more than local interest. If something is done well in the South it must be forsooth southern. It is true that we talk about it's being time something of national importance should be produced from the South, but we either expect such an effort to fail or we are surprised that it does not, and to ask southerner to take counsel of southerner is presumptuous indeed. If we have a large fund to pay for a series of lectures or a survey or for expert work, we find someone outside of the South who agrees to take special time, pains, energy, and very commendably and successfully gives us a good piece of work. It seems never to occur to us that if money were available, if time and leisure and resources were afforded, the type of effort which our own folk put forth would be far different from the hurried, unappreciated results which are obtained whenever there is free service and emergency task. It is a commonplace to affirm that creative work of quality must be produced in workable atmosphere and with workable tools.

VI

Much more ought to be said. Other factors ought to be discussed. These that have been presented ought to be qualified. It must be remembered of course that the term "the South" is not accurate. There are vast differences between the states and in many instances the differences are growing. But most of all we should hasten to say that not one of these counts against the South need in any sense be a permanent fundamental part of our structural civilization and promise. And the statement of these glaring deficiencies ought to give particular emphasis to the startling assertion that in the face of the limitations that now exist it is entirely possible that the South has within its being much of the supreme quality and potential which the nation needs above all things else at this time. To give evidence that this is true and to set in motion forces which will turn the southern potential into national power will constitute the supreme task of the next few generations.

The usual rebuttal that most of the shortcomings which may be charged to the South are also in some degree found in other states and in other sections amounts to nothing. What we are concerned with is the actual fact of what the South is doing and can do. The only criterion will be results. We are tired, eternally tired, of

limitations. Tired of wrong impressions, tired
of the defense complex and mechanism, tired of
unending ridicule, tired of taking second and
third and fourth rate places in achievement,
tired of undeveloped potential, tired of lack of
opportunity, tired of complacency, ignorance,
poverty, and all the paradoxes that now flower
out of a soil which can produce better. Anyone
can add up the five counts which we have enumerated and see the impossibility of ever hoping
for distinguished achievement and service so
long as these conditions last. A full expectation
under these circumstances is ridiculous and im-
moral. The wonder is that the South has done
so much as it has. And the story of its achievement both in its regional rebuilding and in its
contribution of outstanding individuals in the
nation is the greatest possible evidence of its
possibilities and of the critical need for a spiritual
revolution throughout the Southland.

We have not mentioned some of the commonly
discussed handicaps. We have not referred to
the old tendency to render judgment upon individual and creative effort only in relation to
family standing. We have not discussed the
misunderstanding of one class by another, and
other specific factors. We have referred only
indirectly to the handicap of race. We have not
taken into consideration the economic history of
the South, and many factors of mediocrity which

were already appearing even before the war between the states. These we believe are well on
the road to their place in the historical record of
the South of other days. Nor have we enumerated under each of the general deficiencies
discussed the outstanding beginnings looking
already in the direction of new days. There is
ample evidence to show that the South can
evolve its situation. Certain it is that the South
can be brought to make adjustments to meet the
needs of social and economic change. Certain it
is that the South can gain experience and training. The South has already shown that it can
produce and maintain universities and leaders if
it will. It would be absurd to say that because
the South in the past had not produced an atmosphere conducive to creative effort and social
progress it therefore would always be so limited.
And to affirm that the South will not in the
future give adequate reward and recognition to
its leaders would be at once for the South to set
upon itself the seal of inferiority. And the South
has no inclination to do this.

After all, however, is it possible that the South
has something to offer besides its determination
and its ability to eliminate the common deficiencies which all Southerners must agree now
exist, and its will to develop its resources, human
and physical? This itself is, of course, a rich
offering and one that will require heroic efforts

to bring forth. Nevertheless I do not believe that any fair student of the South, adding up and analyzing his accurate data on the subject, can come to any other conclusion than that it can be done. Looking forward, then, to the time when the southern civilization, freed from its self-imposed impassable barriers, shall have created favorable situations, what else is there which the South may offer to the nation at large in addition to the development of its own potential? What is there in its groups from mountain crag to shores of sand which might contribute to a recreating epos? Is there in the spiritual mode, religious zeal, demagogic appeal, stubborn individualism, ethnic unity, heroic pride, adolescent combativeness, imaginative romance, something which exists in abundance in the rough, which the South and the Nation need to mine and refine? There is much evidence to show that there is. The Nation needs some sort of renaissance of intellectual conviction, spiritual rejuvenation and stable morality that does not rattle with superficial verbiage. Shorn of the glory of its introverted social personality and its objective material limitation, what may the South not offer in its newer day? To turn this southern potential into national power is a southern promise, the spirit of which is foretold in the stories of pioneers presented in this volume.

WOODROW WILSON

*A Challenge to the
Fighting South*

BY

GERALD W. JOHNSON

WOODROW WILSON

The Epos of Woodrow Wilson came to a climax so thunderous that it has absorbed attention almost to the complete exclusion of all that preceded it. An article on Woodrow Wilson without reference to the war, or to the League of Nations, may seem to many readers as preposterous as an essay on Agamemnon without reference to the siege of Troy. This is unfortunate, for by the absorption of the President into the Internationalist, the United States and particularly the South loses a figure of outstanding social significance. The Wilson in the Hall of the Clock at Versailles may have been merely a projection of the Wilson in the White House, and the Wilson in the State House at Trenton, and the Wilson in the President's house at Princeton; but his significance in the palace of the French kings is almost entirely unrelated to his significance in the houses built by the people which he occupied in the United States.

A leader of American democracy as dictator of a European peace congress was admittedly an anomaly. Mr. Wilson's presence at Versailles was due to a combination of circumstances unparalleled in history, and a combination which we are permitted to hope we shall never see again. It was not in any sense due to the orderly development of the social consciousness of any people that Mr. Wilson was called upon to play his part upon the European stage. He was thrust upon that stage by forces entirely uncontrollable by the people of the United States, or by any other single nation. He was selected to be President of the United States by the deliberate choice of the people of the United States. He was selected to be the most conspicuous figure at the Peace Conference by a destiny which the people of the United States could neither foresee nor control.

As a social force of significance to democracy, his career before the war is therefore much more important than his career after the storm had burst. To devote attention exclusively to Wilson, the toy of destiny, is to lose sight of a man who expressed with singular clearness and felicity the social consciousness of his time. The nation can ill afford to suffer such a loss. To the South it is desperately heavy, for at this moment of its great expansion, materially and intellectually, it requires as never before careful study of the counsel of all its conspicuously able leaders. It is well worth the while of the South to scrutinize closely the record of this man irrespective of his attitude as an internationalist and to consider to what extent his leadership was effective in the South in matters not pertaining to the war and its aftermath.

It is no part of the purpose of this paper to review in detail the economic and political ideas of Woodrow Wilson. Partisan controversialists have so completely befogged that record that it will tax the resources of able historians for years to get at the truth. Much of it, indeed, is irrelevant to a discussion of the man as a social pioneer. It is intended here to consider rather the underlying faith that was the basis of his actions and to compare it with the underlying faith that seems to be the basis of the social policy of the section that produced Woodrow Wilson. About this, there is little obscurity. As long as the history of the United States is studied, men will doubtless continue to differ about the effectiveness of Wilson's domestic policy, as they will certainly differ about the effectiveness of his foreign policy. As to what he did, it is far too early to dogmatize, but as to what he intended to do there is not much dispute.

There is a consistency in this record that is not only easily traced, but that is so conspicuous that it is impossible to miss it. From the time of his assault on the eating clubs at Princeton to the time of his appeal to the Italian people over the head of Orlando, Woodrow Wilson maintained his faith, not in the righteousness only, but in the efficacy of democracy. In "The Road Away

from Revolution," almost his last public utterance, he ascribed the Russian debacle to the
fact that "The lives of the great mass of the
Russian people contained no opportunities, but
were hemmed in by barriers against which they
were constantly flinging their spirits, only to fall
back bruised and dispirited." This conception of
the common people as constantly flinging their
spirits against the barriers which hem them in, is
surely as high an expression of the democratic
ideal as ever was uttered. Grant that the people
are battering at their barriers, and idealism is
not only justified, but becomes the sole rational
philosophy.

Can it be seriously maintained, though, that
any such conception is held by the existing
leadership of any section of the country? Since
the South is the specific subject of these essays,
confine the inquiry to the South. If Southern
leaders actually believed that the great mass
of the common people of the section are flinging
their spirits against the barriers that hem them
in, where would be the excuse for timidity, for
time-serving opportunism, for obscurantism and
reaction? Such faults and failures of leadership
are inconsistent with a profound belief that the
people are surging against the barriers that
restrain them from the freer and nobler life of
the idealist's dreams.

* * *

The decade since 1914 has been a decade of disillusionment the world over. Perhaps never since Jean-Jacques first inflamed the idealists of France has the intellectual response to the concept of democracy been feebler or more uncertain than it is at present. Passionate enthusiasm is always with the opposition, and democracy is now the party in power.

It is conceivable that the future historian may set down the year 1914 as the high tide of democracy; for ever since its assumption of complete control of the world assaults upon it have been increasing in frequency and vigor. But in 1914 Wilsonian idealism had not yet received a single real body-blow. If Wilson's leadership had ever been effective in his native section one would reasonably expect to find it effective at the moment of its highest power in the rest of the country.

What are the facts? At the Baltimore convention in 1912 the South put up a tremendous fight for the nomination of Oscar W. Underwood, although Wilson received some of its delegates. At the election in November of that year Wilson actually polled a smaller number of votes than Bryan had polled in 1896 in the states of Virginia, North Carolina, South Carolina, Georgia, Mississippi, Louisiana, Texas, Tennessee, Missouri and Arkansas, and a smaller number than Bryan had polled in 1900 in Alabama. Every one of those states showed a material gain in population between 1900 and 1910, and the figures cannot have been affected by the disfranchisement of the negroes since the negroes never voted the Democratic ticket in appreciable numbers. The only possible explanation is that the enthusiasm of the South for Wilson at the height of his popularity never approached its enthusiasm for Bryan at the height of his popularity. In view of the fact that Wilson was generally believed to be a Democrat who could actually win, this refusal of the South to rally to him can be accounted for only on the hypothesis that there existed in the section a profound distaste for the man and his ideas.

In support of that theory there is the record of many Southern representatives and senators during Wilson's administration. Their opposition to the administration was notorious, but they were regularly returned to their seats in Washington by their constituencies. In Georgia, indeed, Thomas E. Watson won on a platform of opposition to Wilsonism more rabid than that of Hoke Smith.

The fact is, no candid observer doubts that if Underwood had been nominated by the Baltimore convention, the South would have voted for him as readily as it voted for Wilson. Perhaps it would have voted more enthusiastically, on account of Underwood's residence in the South.

Now to assume that Oscar W. Underwood and
Woodrow Wilson thought alike because they
were both called Democrats would be as fatuous
as to assume that the last of the czars and Lenine
thought alike because they were both called
Nicholas. Mr. Underwood's social concepts
may or may not be the prevailing mode of
thought in the South. The point is, the very
willingness of the South to vote for either man
proves that Mr. Wilson's concepts did not at
that time dominate it. The fact that it was
willing to return to Washington time after time
men who had opposed Mr. Wilson's social program at every step is proof that it was at best in-
different about the success of that program at
the moment when the rest of the country came
nearest to genuine excitement about it. Mr.
Wilson carried the South in the election of 1912,
but Wilsonism was far from dominating it then.

Woodrow Wilson's faith in democracy was
not, however, incompatible with faith in representative government. His intelligence rejected
the concept of pure democracy as essentially
fallacious. The very nature of the charge most
frequently brought against him is conclusive
proof of his willingness to accept responsibility.
He is accused of autocracy, which is an accusation
never brought against any man whose record in
office is one of indecision and evasion. He
sponsored the doctrine that a President of the

United States is in fact leader of his party as well
as chief executive, which was tantamount to
assumption of responsibility for the legislative,
as well as the executive, record of his administration.

In this he is followed in theory by the South,
but it is becoming more and more the fashion for
political parties and administrative officials to
reject responsibility for any grave decision. The
referendum, first proposed as a weapon for the
people to employ against tyrannous officials,
has recently threatened to become a means of
escape for officials and legislative bodies from the
necessity of making momentous decisions. Nothing in the record of democracy is clearer than
the incapacity of the people to make wise decisions upon complicated questions involving
technical details upon which all but expert
opinion is worthless. Yet more and more frequently legislative bodies are referring such
questions to the people for settlement at the
polls.

This is the antithesis of Wilsonian doctrine.
His bitterest enemies do not deny that he was
courageous, and this policy is the offspring of
timidity in politics. The leadership that acts
and then faces the consequences, instead of
throwing back upon the people the responsibility
that it should assume, is the only true leadership
of representative democracy. The leadership

that ducks and dodges, raising the specious cry of, "Let the people rule," was utterly abhorrent to Wilson, and travesties his spirit when it assumes to wear his colors.

A conspicuous cleavage between the political philosophy of Woodrow Wilson and the political philosophy of the present South is revealed by the war President's iconoclasm. Whatever else the South may be, it is not an image-breaker. Indeed, the most powerful foe of its advancement materially, as well as mentally and morally, has rarely assumed human, or tangible form. It has been rather the dead hand of the past, a fixation of ideas arising from the notion that the Golden Age is behind, and not ahead.

No man of what the Victorian age called "sensibility" can fail to admire the magnificent loyalty of the South, but even loyalty, pushed to excess, becomes a vice. When it goes the length —as it has not infrequently gone in the South— of assuming that everything that has happened since the extinction of the Confederate States of America has been in the nature of degeneration and deterioration, loyalty becomes obscurantism, and a curse to the section it afflicts. A great past is a reproach to a nation that has no future.

After all, what the South thinks of its heroes is of trivial importance by comparison with what the heroes would think of the South, if

they could return to it. It is creditable to the
South that it rejects indignantly the mere
suggestion that it repudiate Robert E. Lee; but
it would be more to the purpose for the section
to bend its energies to making sure that Robert
E. Lee, if he were raised from the tomb, would
not repudiate the South.

Think what the brave and chivalrous gentleman would say if he were told how white women
have been stripped of their clothing and beaten
by a mob of Southern white men wearing masks.
Think of what the just and honorable officer
would say if he were told that negroes have been
hanged without trial in the South because they
were suspected of having poisoned mules! Think
of what the President of Washington College
would say if he were given first the automobile
statistics, and then the educational expenditures
of his native section for the past year! It is no
virtue for us to proclaim vociferously that Lee
is good enough for us. Simple Simon can see
that. What would puzzle Socrates to decide is,
are we good enough for Lee?

That is the sort of question that interested
Woodrow Wilson. He was a historian by profession. He knew the history of this country,
including the South, far better than the average
Southerner knows it; but few men have been less
inclined to make an idol of history and to bow
down before it. His impulse, on the contrary,

was always to strike out in a new direction, to try something that had never been tried before, in the hope of achieving a success that had never been achieved before.

This spirit of adventure, of intellectual pioneering, certainly has not informed the South. It has not been wholly without effect, of course. The hopeful aspect of the situation is the fact that in many of the states below the Potomac there are conspicuous leaders who are Wilson men to the extent of believing in the incessant endeavor to break new paths, to attempt new tasks, if necessary to brave new dangers and to risk new failures. The discouraging aspect is that these leaders are so extremely conspicuous. If there were more of them, they would stand out less prominently.

* * *

The man Wilson was an intellectual. To mention the fact is to classify him as outside the ranks, not in the South alone, but in any section of the country. His profound and intense religious convictions cannot be doubted by anyone who has paid the slightest heed to his utterances and writings, or observed his actions with any sort of understanding; nevertheless, he denied that any department of life is closed to the exercise of reason. Shortly before his death he wrote to an inquirer that he not only believed in the theory of evolution as applied to the origin of man but was amazed that anyone should question it.at this late date.

It seems to be pretty well established that the type of leadership that denies the right of man to employ his reason in every department of life wields greater influence in the South than in any other section of the country. Inferior obscurantists exist in multitudes everywhere, and occasionally one discovers the type in a position of great authority and prestige in other sections. But it is difficult to avoid the concluson that it is in the South that one finds the larger number of formidable rulers, especially in the ecclesiastical and educational realms, who frankly and openly advocate shackling the reason in the presence of what they deem sacred subjects.

The blatant cynicism of the Southern theologian and educator of a certain type in denying the intellectual aspirations of Woodrow Wilson yields nothing to the cynicism of those senators who denied his international aspirations. One of the exquisite ironies of the age is the fact that some of these men, who are openly and shamelessly fighting against the ideal to which Wilson devoted the labor of a lifetime, find no language too blistering to be applied to Senator Lodge and others who fought against the League of Nations, to which Wilson gave about three of his sixty years. To classify such men as followers of Woodrow Wilson would be to admit that they may

> "Compound for sins they are inclin'd to
> By damning those they have no mind to."

* * *

It has not only been possible, in some quarters it has been customary, to make every quality enumerated here the basis of an indictment of Woodrow Wilson. Even his stoutest admirers have deplored one other quality that must be added to the list, namely his combativeness. It may be that Woodrow Wilson was excessive in all his manifestations. None the less, without the very qualities which he is accused of carrying to excess, he never would have been the force that moved the world. "Your goodness must have some edge to it, else it is none" is a dictum accepted by the most conservative. There is no manner of doubt that Woodrow Wilson had an edge, and if in the end it sheared away some indispensable supporters, in the beginning it cut through a vast deal of opposition.

In so far as mere combativeness is concerned, the South suffers no lack of it. A fight can be picked pretty nearly anywhere at pretty nearly any time, if one is determined to have a fight, and is not fastidious as to his opponents or his cause. By proclaiming a certain viewpoint upon the negro question, or upon the Ku Klux Klan, or—in some states—upon partisan politics, one may precipitate any sort of combat, from a vigorous debate up to a clash in which the conclusive arguments are furnished by shotguns and bowie-knives.   On certain questions the South will readily fight all comers in any and every fashion.   But Woodrow Wilson would fight anybody on any question which he felt involved a principle.   The South certainly does not follow him to that extreme.   There is a broad region regarded as tabu by the average Southern leader, and it unfortunately includes some matters that ought to be discussed.

This is conspicuously true of any subject which happens to impinge upon religious dogma. To some extent the consideration that causes Southern leaders to walk warily in the presence of anything that can be tortured into a religious debate is the prudential consideration that it is better to let sleeping dogs lie.   But it is open to question that that is the compelling motive in most cases.   Beyond and behind that is another motive that has no relation whatever to personal safety or to constitutional pacifism. It is the reluctance of amiable and God-fearing men to attack the faith of weaker vessels.   It is a thankless task to demolish illusions and to instill doubts and fears, and there is a widespread belief in the South that it is highly questionable ethically.

Obviously, a consideration of that sort occurs only to men who are thoroughly conscientious and essentially humble-minded. It does not for a moment restrain the fanatic and the ignoramus. The consequence is that too often they are permitted to rage through the land without the raising of a single effective protest. The broader-minded and more intelligent leaders of Southern thought shrug their shoulders and hold their tongues. The stock excuse is, "Oh, well, these fellows no doubt do a certain amount of good among the classes they reach." For this problematical good, therefore, the certain and obvious evil that these men do is permitted. The net result is that the vigor and aggressiveness shown in the South in the field of ethical and religious ideas is almost completely monopolized by the least intelligent and most reactionary leaders in those fields. In such cases the Wilson men are the very men whom Woodrow Wilson would least have desired as followers.

* * *

Above all, and behind all else, Wilson was a spiritual aristocrat. He spent his life fighting the battles of democracy, it is true; but what he strove for was political democracy, economic democracy, perhaps to some extent social democracy. Not for an instant did he adhere to the theory that democracy extends to things of the

spirit. He believed that there are good men and
bad men, and while he would submit to the
political rule of what he regarded as bad men,
he tolerated no suggestion that they had any
right to extend their rule over his spirit. He
bowed to the will of the majority; but so far from
worshipping it, he had for it the most corrosive
scorn when it seemed to him that it willed
wickedness.

Mr. Wilson's intransigent attitude in his last
great fight was due to the fact that in his eyes
the establishment of the League of Nations
transcended all politics and became a spiritual
adventure, where compromise was to him un-
thinkable. Unfortunately for him, others regarded it as nothing of the sort, but a question
of the most practical sort of politics. Thus he
lost his fight, and is accused, not without reason,
of having betrayed his own cause through excess
of zeal.

Be that as it may, he left the world a record
of tremendous strength of conviction. It is
not inconceivable that in so doing he bequeathed
to a skeptical age something more valuable than
the political system he endeavored to establish.
Certainly it is a record of enormous potential
value to the South, if the South chooses to
profit by it. Here was a man of brains and
character who believed that it is the duty of
brains and character to rule the world, or to go

down fighting for empery. What a contrast to the pseudo-aristocracy, that will not soil its white fingers with deeds of violence to no matter what end!

We are prone to forget that "aristocracy" does not mean the existence of a superior class, but the rule of a superior class. He would be a pessimist indeed who would deny that a class superior, not on account of blood, but on account of brains and character, exists in the South; but he would be an optimist equally extreme who would dare to maintain that that class rules in the South. The superior class never has ruled and never will rule except where and when it was willing to fight. The ancient aristocracy that attained and maintained its dominance by means of the sword had a comparatively simple task, which required mainly physical strength and courage. The new aristocracy is faced by a problem infinitely more complex. It must assert and maintain its superiority by means of intellectual and moral weapons. But the fact that the style of warfare has changed does not mean that the fighting is any the less bitter. On the contrary it has, if anything, increased in ferocity, for no Jacquerie in human form ever was as bitter, as relentless, and as tireless as the evil spirits that the intellectual and moral aristocrat has to combat. Villeins and serfs once crushed would not rise again for many years.   But ignorance, bigotry, intolerance, and obscurantism are never weary and never sleep.

They have carved on Woodrow Wilson's tomb no effigy and no inscription, but simply a naked sword.   It is a symbol of magnificent audacity to carve upon the sepulchre of the protagonist of peace.   It recalls the audacity of another suggestion that comes perhaps somewhat too faintly down the centuries: "Think not that I am come to send peace on earth: I came not to send peace, but a sword"!

The South, God knows, has cause to be weary of wars.   The doctrines of pacificism are wondrous sweet to her, still crippled by ancient wounds.   It is no marvel that her leaders are still impressed with the belief that the highest patriotic service they can render is the suppression of strife, the avoidance of disputation, the rigorous ironing out of all dissent.   But that doctrine grows pernicious when concord is purchased at the price of spiritual and moral compromise. The social significance of Woodrow Wilson is the fact that he stands as a tremendous denial of the doctrine that life is so dear and peace so sweet as to be worth purchase at the price of moral and intellectual chains and slavery.

* * *

We call ourselves Wilson men in the South because we gave large majorities to the Demo-

cratic party, and because we are always ready
to cheer an orator's mention of Wilson, as we
cheer his mention of Lee. But in his lifetime
what Lee needed at his back was not orators,
but men-at-arms. What Wilson needed was not
talkers, but fighters. The question has been
raised as to whether the South is worthy of Lee.
Is it any more worthy of Wilson? That question
cannot be answered in words, but only in deeds,
deeds done in the name of Wilson, who was a
fighting man, a man, if you choose, of violence.
If Wilson could speak to the Southerner who
protests his devotion to the ideals of the dead
leader, it is easy to imagine that he might
listen without comment to all the oratory, and
then reply in the words of a hero of an old-
fashioned romance: "Sir, I am waiting for you
to draw."

WALTER HINES PAGE

A Southern Nationalist

BY

ROBERT D. W. CONNOR

WALTER HINES PAGE

By birth and spiritual inheritance Walter
Hines Page was a Southerner; by conviction,
education and intellectual outlook he was a
Nationalist. Born in North Carolina of Southern
pioneer stock, he developed early in life a strong
sense of local attachment which he never lost,
and his last request was that his body be brought
back and laid to rest in the soil from which it
had sprung. Son of an "old line Union Whig,"
who never sympathized with secession, Page
came while still a youth to think of the effort
to establish a Southern Confederacy as a ghastly
mistake. His search for an education which he
could not obtain at home carried him far afield
for a Southern rural boy of the 'seventies, not
geographically so much as intellectually, for it
introduced him into the world of Gildersleeve
and Huxley and Darwinism. Before reaching
maturity he had traveled extensively both in his
own country and in Europe—an almost unprecedented thing for a Southern youth of that
day—and so had immeasurably broadened his
intellectual outlook. Thus before he was twenty-
five years old, "he had outgrown any Southern
particularism with which he had started life.
He no longer found his country exclusively

south of the Potomac: he had made his own the West, the North—New York, Chicago, Denver, as well as Atlanta and Raleigh;"[1] and out of these experiences came that "wide-sweeping Americanism" which was one of his most striking characteristics.

The immediate result, however, was to unfit him for work in the South of the 'eighties, for he had lost touch with his own people and it required but two years of painful experience to demonstrate this fact. From school and travel, Page returned to North Carolina burning with zeal to have a hand in the rebuilding of the old Commonwealth. He found her sitting disconsolate amid the ruins of her former glory, satisfied, as it seemed to him, in the mere nursing of her grievances. To arouse her out of her lethargy—to start her forward on the road of social, economic, and political progress—seemed simple tasks to the eager, optimistic youth. The vehicle which he chose for his purpose was the press, through whose columns he preached with the zeal of a missionary the gospel of universal education, industrial training, farm-ownership, and the development of natural resources. His utterances awakened a ready response in the souls of a few young and eager spirits—all men of the new generation—but the men of the

---

[1] Hendrick, Burton J., "The Life and Letters of Walter H. Page." 2 v. 1922.

'sixties, still the chief spokesmen of the South,
would have none of him.

It must be said, however, that it was not
entirely North Carolina's fault that she and her
brilliant young son did not get along together
better. The young editor, enthusiastic and im-
patient of delay, spared nobody and no thing
that stood in the way of his program. Slashing
away right and left with all the weapons of his
craft, he poured forth a steady torrent of wit,
satire, ridicule and invective against the three
"ghosts" which he believed were strangling
North Carolina, and the rest of the South, in the
grip of dead men's hands,—"The Ghost of the
Confederate dead, the Ghost of religious orthodoxy, the Ghost of negro domination." He saw
in North Carolina a "mummified" community—a
political and social Thothmes II—into whose
dead body it was his mission to breathe the
breath of life. Now, nobody enjoys being the
victim of ridicule, and Page soon found it an
"awfully discouraging business to undertake to
prove to a mummy that it is a mummy." The
grinning old thing seemed very well satisfied to
rest peacefully in its ancestral tomb and pro-
tested loudly against the sacrilegious efforts of
the young Knight of Progress to disturb its
slumbers.

In arousing Thothmes II, Page committed a
capital error, for the mummy which he so mer-

cilessly lambasted was not the real North Carolina, even of the 'eighties, and he should have
allowed it to rest quietly in its sarcophagus.
Page had mistaken the hobgoblins of a dying
civilization for the spirits of a living one; he was
fighting the ghosts of a dead past and didn't
know it. He should have let the dead alone and
devoted his energies and abilities to stimulating
the activities of the living. At the very moment
when he was sighing "for a change in his beloved
South—a change of almost any kind!"—Washington Duke, Julian S. Carr, R. J. Reynolds, and
the Hanes brothers were beginning those tobacco
manufactories; the Holts, the Cannons, and the
Odells were establishing those cotton mills; A. B.
Andrews and R. R. Bridgers were laying those
cross ties and steel rails; the Sprunts were developing that world-wide cotton-export business;
McIver, Alderman, Joyner, Aycock were preaching that gospel of universal education; and Battle
and Winston were reopening the University of
North Carolina for that higher education, all
of which taken together were to result in a very
few years— in Page's own life-time, indeed—in
one of the most remarkable outbursts of industrial and agricultural development, commercial
expansion, and social and educational progress in
the history of any American state.

In other words those men, and hundreds of
others like them, throughout the South, were

doing the very things that Page was talking about, but he did not recognize the fruits of his own gospel. Indeed, how could he know that the loghouse, 20 x 30 feet, in Durham, where Washington Duke and his sons were manufacturing literally with their own hands the tobacco which they peddled through Eastern North Carolina in a ramshackle wagon "drawn by two blind mules," was but the first link in a chain of giant factories which before Page's own generation had passed away was to encircle the globe?

After two years of apparently fruitless effort in the South, therefore, the discouraged editor "cast off the shackles of provinciality for the freedom of cosmopolitanism," i. e., he "went North," leaving North Carolina in the grip of that "mummified aristocracy" which, he modestly laments, "was driving the best talent and initiative from the state."

Entirely too much has been made of Page's querulous plaint that he was not allowed "to work for the old state," and conclusions far wide of the mark have been drawn from it. Does it follow that because an artist can find no market for his wares in a bankrupt community that the community has no appreciation of the work of superior men? Certainly Walter Page had no such thought; on the contrary he was the first to realize (from his own experience) and to point out that the immediate task of the "superior

men" of the South was not the production of
literature but the economic rehabilitation of their
land. Art, music, "a great outburst of literature," all alike await upon freedom, he told
North Carolina's "Literary and Historical Association," in 1912, and "the only real freedom is
economic freedom." "Do you want literature?"
he asked. Then, answering his own question,
he continued:

"Nothing has happened in literature but it admits of
an easy and obvious explanation—after the event. But
I have not found any historian who foretold a time of rich
production. . . . It would be a great satisfaction to know
just when and under what conditions a great outburst
of literature will come in North Carolina. . . . Now I am
going to have the audacity to make such a prediction. . . .
We need only so to preserve and develop our land as to
make it the most famous land in the world and so to use
money in getting riches out of it as to prove that it is
the safest land in the world—and that our countrymen
are the safest people. And do you want literature? With
this result you will have something better than literature;
but literature will come along with the other arts."

Walter Page himself was the best exemplar of
his own philosophy; he threw in his lot as editor
of the *Atlantic Monthly* because it was finan-
cially able to buy the best editorial talent in the
market; he left the *Atlantic Monthly* twelve years
later largely because it was unwilling to assure
him complete economic freedom. The Harkness
Memorial at Yale is probably the most beau-

tiful college building in America, not because Yale appreciates art any more than does the University of North Carolina, but because, dear reader, behind the art of a Rogers are the millions of a Harkness. And don't forget that Grand Opera went to Atlanta just as soon as Atlanta was able to pay for it.

The lesson which Page tried so hard to teach "Issachar" is that the Eli Whitneys, Thomas A. Edisons, Henry Fords, and Seaman A. Knapps must do their work first so as to provide the money, the freedom, and the leisure that are essential to the support and appreciation of the Beethovens, the Rodins, and the Joseph Conrads when they do come. May it not be, then, that in developing thews and sinews of steel and nerves of copper cables, Issachar is not such a stupid ass after all?[2]

Then, too, here comes Page's biographer who writes of his having been forced to "forego his hope of playing a part in rescuing his state from the disasters of the Civil War." But Page's father and younger brothers were under no such compulsion. On the contrary, they found oppor-

[2] See Gerald W. Johnson's "Issachar Is a Strong Ass" in the November *Journal of Social Forces*. "How," asks Mr. Johnson, "does Issachar estimate the value of a man as compared with a cotton mill?" He finds his answer in the fact that, although our British cousins have placed a memorial to Walter Page in Westminster Abbey, "there is no monument to Page in North Carolina." And yet while Mr. Johnson was writing those words, the community in which Walter Page was born was dedicating a $50,000 "Walter Hines Page Industrial School" within a stone's throw of the place of his birth. Can anybody think of a memorial that would have been more pleasing to Walter Page?

tunities all around them for playing such a part
through the improvement of farm lands, the
development of lumber enterprises, the establishment of financial institutions, and the building of railroads, and they remained in the South
to take advantage of these opportunities and to
enroll themselves high among those "builders of
an old commonwealth" of whom Walter Page
himself wrote so appreciatively.

The opportunities were here all right, but
it is no disparagement to the genius or the patriotism of Walter Page to say that he was not
fitted by training or temperament to play a
part in developing them. The South of the
'eighties could not understand or sympathize
with this Nationalist; and this Nationalist had
neither patience nor sympathy with the provincialism of the South. When he came to
realize the fact he simply sought another field
of labor for which he was better equipped. It
was well for both him and the South that he did
so; together, they could never have lived har-
moniously; separated, they came to respect and
love each other.

For Walter Page loved the South. Intellectually a Nationalist, he was spiritually a Southerner. "The Southerner" is the title which he
selected for his "anonymous autobiography,"
and he retained throughout life an affection,
typically Southern, for the state of his birth.

At the close of a brilliant career at the Court of St. James, he found himself thinking not of his many personal successes in diplomacy, nor even of his country's military triumphs, but "of the winter down South;" and when at last he returned to his Southern home to die, his first words, spoken with "a slightly triumphant smile" as his son carried him from the train in his arms, were, "Well, Frank, I did get here after all, didn't I?" And he wrote as far back as 1879, "I shall some day buy a home where I was not allowed to work for one, and be laid away in the soil I love." There can be no doubt on this point; Walter Page was a real "down homer."

But Page did not wear his heart on his sleeve; if there was one specimen of the human race that he more thoroughly detested than any other it was the vociferous "professional Southerner." He never wrote anything finer than his letter on "that queer sect, 'The Excoriators,'" as he dubbed certain Southerners who, he was told, had been "excoriating" him for his criticisms of the South. Page himself preferred to manifest his affection for the South in outspoken criticism of her faults, constructive suggestions for improvements, and in genuine service.

The South of the 'eighties and 'nineties was in mortal danger of being strangled in the grip of a deadening sectionalism, and no voice was raised

in warning so fearless, so far-reaching, and so
stimulating as the voice of this Southern Nationalist. He turned upon her the full light of
truth and spoke with frankness—often brutal
frankness—of her failure to strike out into the
great intellectual, social and spiritual currents of
modern life. The provincial, untraveled South
of the nineteenth century did not realize how far
below the American standard she was in educational and social progress, and it was largely the
voice of Walter Page, ringing clear and distinct
above the clamor of the "Excoriators," that
taught her to see herself as others saw her.

Page refused to look at Southern conditions
and problems through the eyes of a Southerner,
but insisted upon seeing them from the point of
view of a broad and ever-widening Nationalism.
A South, illiterate, unhealthy, poverty-stricken,
was a national peril; therefore, the South must
be encouraged and helped to build schools,
establish boards of health, develop her natural
resources, and make adequate provision for the
social and spiritual welfare of the average man.
He made it a special charge upon himself to
search out philanthropists, publicists, and experts in finance, education, sanitation, and
agriculture whom he might interest in the South,
and the stories of some of his experiences in this
work read like romances. I know of no more
interesting story than that of Page's relations

with Dr. Charles W. Stiles and the Hookworm Commission, nor a more beautiful one than that of his friendship with Dr. Seaman A. Knapp.

It is no under-estimate of his other achievements to say that Page's most enduring work and that for which, I am sure, he would prefer to be held in remembrance, was his work for social progress in the South. Witness the General Education Board, a direct development of the Southern Education Board; the International Health Commission, an outgrowth of the Hookworm Commission which thus turned out to be the beginning of "an enterprise that is the greatest sanitary and health reform of modern times;" and the Farm Demonstration Work of the United States Department of Agriculture, the result, through Page's interest, of Knapp's humble efforts in "one of the cotton states."

I do not mean to claim that Page either originated or developed these great social agencies. To create and develop are jobs for experts, and Page was not an expert in education, in sanitation, or in agriculture; he was rather the statesman, pointing out big social problems for the expert to attack, laying down large policies for the expert to follow, and winning public approval and organizing public support for the expert's work. McIver, Stiles, Flexner, Knapp, struggling against misunderstanding and prejudice, and a vast public indifference, all found in Page's genius and enthusiasm that intellectual stimulus and moral support without which it is doubtful if they could have kept their hands to the plow. Thus, although, he did not create great social agencies, nor direct the details of their development, Page did impress upon them a breadth of view, a largeness of vision, and a liberality of policy which in a great measure account for their success.

Typical of Page's methods and of their results was his relation to the educational awakening of his native state. Varying only in details, the story can be duplicated in any Southern state, but North Carolina is selected as an illustration for obvious reasons.

Public education in North Carolina was one of Page's earliest interests and at the very beginning of the modern movement he threw himself into the thickest of the fight, not as an educational expert, of course, but as an educational agitator and statesman. Charles D. McIver, Edwin A. Alderman, Walter H. Page—"these were the three guardsmen of this new battle for the elevation of the white and black men of the South." While McIver and Alderman were working out the professional details of the movement, it was Walter Page, then "living far away in the North," who kept them to their self-appointed tasks by "pumping them full of courage and enthusiasm." When the cause began to lag, it was Page who furnished its rallying cry—"The

Forgotten Man"—"which lived in the popular mind and summed up, in a way that a thousand speeches could never have done, the great purpose for which the best people of the state were striving." When others were timidly ready to compromise on "a partially free system of education," it was Page who formulated the big liberal policy which alone can solve the South's educational problem,—"a free public school system generously supported by public sentiment and generously maintained by both state and local taxation" in which "a child of either sex may begin its education at a public school and pursue it through the State University without charge." When the movement had once got under way, it was Page who realized the need of thorough organization and brought to its support first the Southern Education Board, of which he was "the most active worker," and later the General Education Board which at once became his "chief outside interest."

I do not think it possible to overestimate the importance of Page's contributions to this educational movement in North Carolina, for I am sure that the experts,—McIver, Joyner, Brooks, Coon, Foust—will bear me out in the assertion that their work in its fullest scope would have been impossible but for the influence, moral and financial, which Walter Page was largely responsible in bringing to their support.

Let it be remembered, too, that education was but one of Page's interests in the South. They embraced the whole program of social progress, including political reform, agricultural development, improved sanitary and health conditions, the uplift of the black man, the cultivation of better race relations between blacks and whites, all of which he considered legitimate functions of the democratic state.

In other words, Page sought to displace in the South the old aristocratic concept of government, which saw the state simply as a policeman concerned chiefly with courts and constables and prisons, with the democratic concept which sees the state as a beneficent social agent with its chief social emphasis on farms and workshops and homes; which recognizes its obligation to promote the physical well-being of its people and to protect them from the attacks of disease; which concerns itself less in the size and wealth of its towns and cities than in developing them into centers of health and beauty, social comfort and economic security; which reclaims its waste places, restores its forests, conserves its resources, and constructs durable highways; which endeavors to build up "a more complete and enduring rural civilization, where strong and vigorous manhood is reared and where the rarest and purest forms of womanhood are in bloom;" which recognizes no higher duty than the protection of

childhood, the education of youth, and the conservation of manhood and womanhood; a state
not only in which no man is so high that the
law of the common good cannot reach him, but
also, in the words of Charles B. Aycock, that
higher and finer thing, a state in which "no man
is so low that it shall not reach down to him to
lift him up if may be and set him on his feet
again and bid him Godspeed to better things."

There are, I think, a thousand indications
that the South is beginning to grasp this concept
of the state. For instance, in the year 1924,
alone, North Carolina spent on the construction
of highways, the care of mental and physical
defectives, the conservation of health, the improvement of living conditions on the farm and in
the home, the distribution of good books to the
people, the salvaging of physical and spiritual
derelicts, the tender care of childhood, public
education, and other forms of social work, more
money than the total expenditures of the state
were for all purposes during the thirty years
from 1868 to 1897;[3] and all this work is carried on
at public expense, both state and local, through
a system of officials, boards, commissions, juvenile courts, hospitals, and schools most of which
did not exist when Page stirred the conscience of
the state with his plea for "The Forgotten Man."

[3] Date of Page's address on "The Forgotten Man."

CHARLES BRANTLEY AYCOCK
Epic Builder of Education

BY

EDWIN A. ALDERMAN

CHARLES BRANTLEY AYCOCK

The people of North Carolina have chosen to put aside their cares and businesses this day[1] for a simple and noble process of thought—the enshrining in their hearts and memories of a man whom they grew to love; a fellow citizen who incited them to lofty action; and of a public servant who modestly, but radiantly, served the interests of his people and mankind. This outpouring of a great people with every mournful ceremony of affection and remembrance is very impressive proof that North Carolinians do not will that the renown of their great servants shall hereafter suffer neglect but rather that all that art and genius can do shall be done to hand on to other ages the bronze or marble images of those who dreamed wide dreams of social perfection and peace and struggled manfully for their realization.

We are giving thought today not to the death of Charles Brantley Aycock, for such as he can never quite be imprisoned with the dead, but to his steadfast and romantic life which shall endlessly endure, inspire, and teach. It is in such high ways that great states grow to maturity in

[1] An address delivered before the North Carolina Education Association at Raleigh, March 13, 1924.

intelligence and discernment, pay homage to character and make solemn public declaration that a life of pure purpose carried forward usefully constitutes in this Republic a patent of nobility which time shall not permit to lapse or posterity to terminate.

I am grateful for the privilege and honor accorded to me to preside at this memorial meeting. It is not possible for one born and bred of this soil to stand in this presence without a big stir of emotion. It will be a memory to cherish and keep green throughout all life. It is not my part or purpose to attempt to present to you today a formal memorial address, but rather to speak as one who knew Charles Aycock when both of us had youth and walked together in the early morning of life; to seek to re-create his gallant figure in some faint measure for the eyes of those who did not know him; and to pick out for contemplation some of the saliencies of his character, which thus move a great people to set him up so grandly at the center of their life.

I had sight of Charles Aycock for the first time in the fall of 1878, forty-six years ago, at the University of North Carolina, in the little academic village of Chapel Hill, which both of us were learning to love with a love which lasted him to his death and shall last me to mine. He was a senior and I a freshman; he was a "Phi" and I a "Di." He was country born and bred and

I city born and bred, with the understanding that my city, though the most populous we then had, must not be thought of as a thronging Babylon but as a very charming and cultivated little Southern town. These were estranging circumstances, but we soon came to know each other. He was plainly rural to the ordinary eye, but only a dullard could fail to perceive a certain distinction in his presence, a certain authority in his manner, and a certain significance in the very cadences of his voice. Through the mists of memory, I see him standing clear against the stark simplicity of that environment—a figure of vividness and strength, the bony structure of his great projecting forehead, blue eyes that had in their depths speculation and aspiration, and, now and then, a flash such as warriors have in the hour of battle; a mouth scornful of weakness and set in grim lines of pride and purpose—about the whole personality a soaring quality, a lift of the head, a lift of the voice as one not bound to the earth and the things of the earth, but aware and wistful of better things that are not seen and fiercely bent upon their attainment.

It is a common and beautiful custom for those of us clad in the sober russet of middle life or advancing years, to think with emotion of the old collegiate quadrangle where were housed, in Cardinal Newman's phrase, "the bright colored garments of a youth apparently endless." But

I take leave to say that there could not have been in all the world a better place for the tutelage of the spirit and the nourishment of the mind than Chapel Hill in that day of small but serene things. We were all of us poor. We knew each other and called each other by name. Student ambitions tended almost entirely toward law, politics, or scholarship. The tocsin soon to sound the birth of the great industrial awakening, which was to transform our civilization from an agricultural into an industrial democracy, had not yet quite sounded. Our standards demanded character, not possessions. Loyalty and courage were the virtues that touched our imaginations, and on the pathway of all of us lay the light reflected from the patient faces of our fathers and mothers who had outfaced war and its sufferings and poverty and its trials, but had not failed to keep their honor bright and their names without stain. The one thing we learned more valuable, perhaps, than all the learning of the meagre and struggling University, and which the bronze figure of Charles Aycock will proclaim to generations of youth, was the beauty that lies in annexing oneself in youth to some large truth and some just cause with the knowledge that though we fail, the cause will not fail but goes marching on, and our souls march on with it, because we believed in it and gave it service.

It was my good fortune, as soon as I entered
as a worker into the world of men, to find myself a fellow citizen with Charles Aycock in a
small, sincere, dignified, progressive community,
not given to over-praise or over-blame, but level-
headed, equable, just, and wonderfully kind.
Goldsboro was almost as well adapted to train
the young citizen as Chapel Hill had been to
train the young scholar. Aycock was busy building a home and laying, by honest labor, the
foundations of his great professional reputation.
I was learning, to my astonishment, the fateful
significance of education in a scheme of self
government. We sometimes walked and talked
together about the things that seem significant
when life lies before, about men and affairs, and
all the framework of the land. These contacts
revealed to me that Aycock, like Lincoln, was
not primarily a logician or a polemic but a poet
and a man of letters. I do not mean that he
actually wrote verse, but I do mean that his
mind worked best through images created by his
imagination, and that he loved and was deeply
moved by beauty—

"Beauty, old, yet ever new,
Eternal voice and
Inward Word,"

without which our democracy shall surely perish.
   Listen to him, in his maturity, preaching to
cool, appraising North Carolina audiences the

doctrine that growth, in state or individual life, means sacrifice and suffering. "No man reaches the highest mountain peak until he has bruised his knees and scrambled over boulders and fallen into gulches in his way up to the height. Indeed, before he reaches there, his head shall split with aching, his back shall break and the nails on his fingers shall be torn out by the roots as he pulls himself up the rugged way. But when he does reach the top, the world lies at his feet and the pathway seems to him no longer difficult. The boulders are out of sight, gently covered by the grass that grows by the wayside, while the flowers burst into the beauty of the eternal morning. The struggle upward is worth the cost, and without the cost would not be worth while."

There are offered here no tabulated statistics—no major and minor premises and conclusions, but just pictures, such pictures as the Great Teacher and Democrat of us all, envisaged long ago in Syrian fields and, hanging forever in our minds, excel all others in wisdom and beauty.

We talked of education now and then. My own mind at that time was just possessing itself of the profound and exciting conviction which has been the moulding force in my life, not then a dogma of common belief—that every human being has the same right to be educated that he has to be free. One of the cherished hopes of my heart, my fellow citizens, is that I may have dropped some thought into the soil of his creative mind, then engrossed in the law and the reason thereof, about the free education of all the people as the foundation of a democracy and the highest function of an enlightened Commonwealth, that made clearer for him, however dimly, the vision which, in later years, he carried in such knightly fashion to the citizenry of North Carolina; which he caused to be translated into political action, and so laid the foundation for his native state to bulk larger in American consciousness than she has done in the two hundred and sixty years of her existence as a self-governing community.

The story of the way in which Charles Aycock, self-forgetful and thrilling with purpose and energy, went to a tax-hating people and convinced them that ignorance is no remedy for anything; that taxation, though it may be a curse, when used wisely and sanely is the greatest beneficent contrivance of civilization to achieve high public ends, and that faith in trained men and women is the supreme tenet of American democracy, this story has become a political legend. Whenever and wherever that perennial struggle is going on, that tale is told. Only the other day I saw fit to tell the tale over again to the General Assembly of Virginia and to say that, though political parties are forever dying, no permanent disaster ever befell a leader or a platform of progress in education, and, further, that I was coming here to help set up a statue to a friend of mine who had the coolness and foresight and sagacity to tie his policy to man and freedom, to the training of the sons and daughters of all the people, rich and poor, black and white, and, lo! had become for all time a popular hero to a great and progressive Commonwealth.

And so we come to the core of this whole matter, to the significance of this hushed assembly, to the spiritual reason for this majestic monument, done by a master's hand, with its lofty serenity, its stately repose, and its power to lift the hurrying throngs moving about its base to unselfish thoughts and generous impulses. I think Charles Aycock may well be accounted a man of good fortune—fortunate in his ancestry; fortunate in his birthplace and in the age in which he was born; fortunate in his profession and in his public work; thrice fortunate in his death, with his powers unwasted, his form erect and vital, his very passing from mortal eyes a glorious gesture of patriotic devotion.

There was a pleasing versatility about Charles Aycock. He had interest in many things. He loved nature and he loved books. There was joy to him in the procession of the seasons, the greenness of springtime, the austere splendor of autumn, the witchery of white winter, and there was delight to him in the companionship of the great masters of thought and phrase potent in his age, like Tennyson, and Carlyle and Macaulay. But he most loved men and men loved him. This love of his for men was no form of superlative amiability and inexhaustible sweetness of temper. He was quite equal to putting fools and selfseekers in their places, for his love for men had its roots deep down in the potency and mystery of our common life and destiny on this earth. "Thou shalt love the Lord thy God. Thou shalt love thy neighbor as thyself." This is the summation of Democracy as well as Christianity. They both are counsels of perfection to upward struggling humanity. They both are far from ruling the world of men, and just now both have fallen on evil days, but they forever gleam, invite, and beckon, and we poor mortals build monuments to those strong souls who follow their light and will not turn aside. They become mankind's liberal heroes.

Aycock not only loved masses of men philosophically, but the individual man was near to his curiosity and his interest. Many great liberal souls like Thomas Jefferson and Woodrow Wilson have loved mankind and would have been willing to go to the stake to protect all men against tyranny and oppression, but they were not particularly interested in any individual, ordinary Tom Jones whom they met along the roadside. Aycock loved Tom Jones on the road-

side, especially if it was a North Carolina roadside and a Tar Heel Tom Jones, and was by him
beloved; and this relation put into his hands the
flashing weapon of sympathy and understanding
by which he hewed his way to usefulness and
power. Tom Jones after all is a very interesting
fellow. Jesus Christ loved to talk to him along
the byways and the highways. Socrates spent all
day, every day, talking to Tom and evoking from
his contacts a noble philosophy of life. Lincoln
loved to "rassle" with him, and John Marshall,
though he denied him ability to govern himself or others wisely, liked nothing better than to
pitch horse shoes with him in the tavern yard.

Aycock was an ambitious man, but he did not
lend his voice to the mob or find contentment
with tawdry public acclaim or give ear to popular
frenzy. He was the very antithesis of the dema-
gogue. He went out among the people in an interesting moment of social assertion, and there
came to him a mounting enthusiasm that so
expressed itself in tone, gesture, manner and
substance, as to move strongly any body of men.
Like Gladstone, what he received from his
hearers as vapor, he returned to them as rain.
There lived in him the power to kindle sympathy
and trust in himself through the might of his own
affection and single-mindedness, and when this
was achieved, he told men not what they might
be then howling for and wanting to hear, but

what they ought to think and do. That is leadership—a rare but glorious compound of intelligence, courage, sympathy, and patience, tipping,
as with fire, the tongue of him who possesses it.

George William Curtis loved to point out how
Lord Chatham's glowing form, when he stood at
the head of England organizing her victories by
land and sea and telling in Parliament their
splendid story, was Britain's self, and the roar of
British guns and the proud acclamation of
British hearts all around the globe flashed and
thundered in his eloquence.

Charles Aycock became the Lord Chatham of
a re-awakened American state. No guns thundered and flashed in his eloquence, but silver
bells of hope rang in the hearts of thousands of
his fellow citizens, and weak purposes became
strong resolves that all children should be given
an opportunity to make the most of themselves
in the world in which they lived.

States like individuals have moods of mind.
It was Aycock's good fate to find his birthplace
in the mood of greatness on the eve of "burgeon-
ing," to use his own word, into its intensest expression of power, and hospitable to every in-
timation of liberalism and progress. I venture to
assert that the period stretching between 1890
and the present constitutes North Carolina's
true golden age, for it has been the age when her
old men, beaten in war, used patience and mag-

nanimity, when her young men, disciplined in self-denial and nurtured on lofty pride, developed a passion for constructiveness, a genius for sympathy, and a method of education. It has been the age when all the people, young and old and high and low, have discovered in unity and community effort the secret of social growth and by wise and steady use of the new instrument have placed North Carolina in the front rank of American states in industrial vigor, in educational advancement, in idealistic fervor.

In his crusading form, North Carolina beheld herself pleading with herself to lay aside provincialism and narrowness of view, to think continentally, not parochially, and to clothe herself in the beautiful raiment of a modern state. To the people who heard him, he was an incarnation and an allegory of themselves lifted up into great powers by the might of genius and the strength of ten. What Aycock desired and pleaded for, and what others before and after him pleaded for in that great historic moment in North Carolina has now in amazing measure come to pass. The "epic of democracy" which he chanted so eloquently and personified so vividly, seems to be at hand.

The elder ones among us recall how North Carolina once symbolized to her sister states an unhasting and immobile community of gentle manners and quiet, homely ways, not avid of the limelight, much enamoured of contentment and dignity, a patient community suspicious of progress, sensitive to injustice and capable of a terrible, stern sort of courage if, perchance, battle and struggle were the order of the time. I have been away from my birth state for a quarter of a century, and as I believe that some of these qualities are very real virtues, I trust that some of them still reign here. They do not now, however, define North Carolina to the outside world. A correctness of estimate as to social needs, a genius for social coöperation, a resolute way of gaining quick action, an enthusiasm for the future, a far-ranging vision of social achievement and social control, an immeasurable pride and ambition—this is North Carolina to the Republic today. The most serene and detached of the sisterhood of states has become a gadfly to the states that lag, a beacon light to those that aspire. And this is such a destiny for his beloved State as Charles Aycock dreamed of and fought for. Democracy, like a man's character, is always in danger. New perils will surround, new dangers threaten, new pitfalls lie in wait for this new social structure you are building here, now so assured and jubilant. Let us have faith that we are setting up today in the Capitol Square, which is becoming for me a sort of outdoor Pantheon of old and dear friends, in yonder bronze image, a figure of simple greatness around

which men may repair in any hour of wrong
direction, of difficulty or disaster, to take counsel
how they may tread the path of sympathy and
courage and use the method of love and patience
to win the heart and gain the support of the
intelligent and wilful democracy of the future.

I had sight of my old friend, then Governor of
North Carolina, for the last time in Athens,
Georgia, in the year 1902. He was closing an
address to a great educational conference in
these words, still speaking in pictures—"God
give us patience and strength that we may work
to build up schools that shall be as lights shining
throughout the land—ten, fifty, a thousand
candle-power. Behind this movement for the
education of the children of our land there stands
the One who said 'Let there be light.'" I still
remember the pride I had in the reflection that
Charles Brantley Aycock had travelled a long
distance from the cotton fields of Wayne to that
hour. Authority and high station sat upon him
becomingly and in his mien dwelt the repose
and dignity of a leader and ruler of men. Instinct with action and passion he was about his
old task of moving men to higher horizons of
thought and conduct with apt word and per-
suasive reason. What John Milton once sang
of Samson in his great poem, the sweet voices of
good fame will forever sing of the great popular
advocate of North Carolina who wrought such

magic for his people in the day of their proud determination and their new glory.

> "Nothing is here for tears, nothing to wail
> Or knock the breast; no weakness, no contempt,
> Dispraise, or blame; nothing but well and fair,
> And what may quiet us in a death so noble."

SEAMAN A. KNAPP

Pioneer in Southern Agriculture

BY

JACKSON DAVIS

SEAMAN A. KNAPP

"Seventy years of preparation for seven years of work," said Dr. Wallace Buttrick of the General Education Board, in speaking of Dr. Seaman A. Knapp's great service in developing the Farm Demonstration Work. The late Walter Hines Page in his unbounded love and enthusiasm for the South said of it, "This is the greatest single piece of constructive educational work in this or in any age." The State Superintendent of Education for Virginia in a memorial service voiced his feeling in a paraphrase of Scripture, "There was a man sent from God, whose name was Seaman A. Knapp." And the sober judgment of those who have followed the development of American country life through all its phases is that Dr. Knapp was our greatest agricultural statesman.

It was in no sense a disparagement of Dr. Knapp's other achievements that Dr. Buttrick referred to his seventy years as a preparation for his life work. It was only to give emphasis to the supreme importance of the Demonstration Work, which came naturally out of Dr. Knapp's rich and varied experience, which played the fundamental part in the educational revival of the South, led to a nation-wide extension service for rural life through the State Agricultural Colleges,

and which has been studied and adopted in a
modified form in several European countries.
Dr. Knapp had to his credit a long list of achievements, of which any man might be proud.

He was born December 16, 1833, in Essex
county, New York, not far from Lake Cham-
plain, his father a physician and a man of fine
sense and culture. His mother was a Seaman of
New England Quaker ancestry. He was graduated from Union College in 1856 with Phi Beta
Kappa honors. Here he came under the influence
of the president, Dr. Eliphalet Nott, a famous
teacher and a pioneer in his interest in the natural sciences. He married in August of the
same year Miss Maria Hotchkiss, who was
associated with him as teacher and assistant
manager of a preparatory school in New York,
Fort Edward Collegiate Institute. After ten
years they took charge of a girls' school at Poult-
ney, Vermont. He humorously referred to it as
a select school, "for," he said, "we selected all
who would come." Here he met with an accident
which threatened to leave him a cripple for life.
Broken in health, his physicians advised him to
go west and follow an outdoor life, thinking he
could not live more than a year. In 1865 he
accordingly went to Iowa and became a successful farmer. For a time he preached in the little
church in Vinton, Iowa. He began to edit an
agricultural paper, became a state lecturer, then

a teacher and finally, president of the State Agricultural College at Ames, Iowa. He wrote the bill for the establishment of an agricultural experiment station in each state, which was finally with few modifications enacted into law in 1887. In Iowa he was fighting the good fight for better agriculture along with such men as Henry Wallace and James Wilson. In advocating this bill he said: "What can one or two stations on the Atlantic Coast do towards educating half a continent in the broad domain of agriculture? As well might a single cannon, planted on Bunker Hill, defend the seaboard cities of the Nation from the combined attack of the navies of the world."

In 1884 he went to Louisiana to direct the development of a large area of land in which a number of his friends in Iowa were interested. He saw the possibilities of this land, selling at that time for about $1.00 an acre, and he introduced the cultivation of upland rice, which has brought prosperity to large areas of Louisiana, Arkansas, and Texas. It was in developing this region that Dr. Knapp hit upon the demonstration method of teaching adult farmers. Many of those attracted to the region became discouraged and left. He, therefore, chose some of the best farmers from Iowa and other states and induced them to come in and demonstrate good farming in strategic centers. The results were immediate.

The new-comers decided to settle, and this part of Southwest Louisiana is now one of the most prosperous portions of the state. Dr. Knapp said "We then learned the philosophy and the power of agricultural demonstration."

Having established the rice industry on a firm basis, Dr. Knapp was invited by Secretary Wilson to become special adviser for the South in the U. S. Department of Agriculture. In this capacity he went on trips to the West Indies, the Philippines, Japan, and India to study rice culture and to ascertain the varieties best suited for this Southern region.

With this record behind him, surely he had earned a rest from his labors, but instead, at the age of seventy, he was called to his life-work. Out in western Texas the Mexican boll-weevil had suddenly appeared and was advancing in a steady march eastward across the heart of the great cotton producing area. It destroyed millions of dollars' worth of cotton, but the ruin was not confined to the farmers alone. Merchants, bankers, business houses of all sorts, saw their profits vanishing. The people were panic-stricken. Prosperous little towns became like deserted mining camps. The U. S. Department of Agriculture was appealed to for aid. James Wilson, then Secretary, naturally turned to his old friend, Dr. Knapp, as the person best qualified to meet this emergency.

Dr. Knapp went to Terrell, Texas, in 1903, just in advance of the boll weevil. The story is told that a farmer in a pessimistic tone asked him, "Well, what have you brought us?" "Not a thing," replied Dr. Knapp. "Any scheme of relief that is not based on self help is like sending a man to hold up a sick calf. After a while they both get tired and fall down together." He then persuaded a group of citizens to provide an indemnity fund for a farmer who would undertake to follow the directions he gave in the cultivation of his land. Mr. Walter Porter agreed to conduct the demonstration farm. Following Dr. Knapp's directions, given on his visits every two weeks, Mr. Porter cleared $700 on his demonstration field. Dr. Knapp found that he could not destroy the boll weevil, but he soon destroyed the panic, stabilized farming and business in the stricken area and laid the foundations for a more prosperous and diversified agriculture. He began with cotton and demonstrated that it could be grown under boll weevil conditions by the selection of early-maturing varieties, by better preparation and cultivation of the soil. Then he turned to corn and cowpeas and other crops which he showed could be grown successfully. The farmers conducting these demonstrations, as they were called, found themselves raising food and feed supplies to meet their own needs, and still able to raise profitably a smaller amount of cotton as a cash crop. Then they gave attention to leguminous crops to build up the fertility of the soil. With this system they were better off than when they had grown cotton alone and bought all of their supplies. Dr. Knapp convinced the Texas farmer that he could grow corn as cheaply as the farmer in Iowa. The way was now clear. Secretary Wilson placed $40,000 of government funds at Dr. Knapp's disposal and the Farm Demonstration Work was inaugurated throughout the boll weevil area.

But the work was not to be confined to this area. Perhaps the most remarkable effect of it was its influence upon public education in the South. Beginning with a conference at Capon Springs, West Virginia, in 1898, there had been held each year a series of conferences of representative people with a group of public-spirited men of the North who desired to assist the Southern people in the great task of public education. The leading spirit of these conferences was Mr. Robert C. Ogden, and there were associated with him such men as Charles D. McIver, Governor Aycock of North Carolina, E. A. Alderman, Charles W. Dabney, P. P. Claxton, Wickliffe Rose, Hollis B. Frissell, Wallace Buttrick, Walter H. Page, and others. They organized the Southern Education Board, which played an important part in enlisting the entire weight of Southern opinion in the task of universal education.

Then in 1902, Mr. John D. Rockefeller established and endowed the General Education Board. While not limited in any way, one of the principal objects in the establishing of this Board was the assistance of education in the South. Dr. Wallace Buttrick, the secretary and executive officer, set out to discover the best way of doing it. He was already widely known and greatly beloved in the South, because of his magnetic personality and his wise understanding of the social and economic questions underlying Southern life. He knew that, while industry was making rapid strides, the schooling of the great majority of the children of the South would be limited to the country schools, and that these schools could be no better than the economic wealth produced from the soil would support. The average annual earnings of persons engaged in agriculture in some of the Southern states was as low as $150, as compared to $1,000 for Iowa. The people were interested in education, but they did not have the rural wealth to support the schools they desired. Various schemes of teaching agriculture to the young people in school were proposed and rejected.

By a coincidence Dr. Buttrick happened in Texas and heard of Dr. Knapp's work. President David F. Houston of the State A. & M.

College said to him, "There are two universities here in Texas—one is at Austin; the other is Dr. Knapp."

Dr. Buttrick lost no time getting acquainted with this "new university." He found in it the way to bring about a revolution in Southern agriculture, on which to base the substantial improvement in rural education. Dr. Buttrick first met Dr. Knapp in President Houston's home. The story is told that for dinner there was a pie of superlative excellence made by Dr. Houston's mother-in-law. In the discriminating appreciation and praise bestowed upon it by both guests she divined the fact that they, like herself, had both been born and reared in the so-called "pie belt." They at once established a common background for a friendship that meant much for Southern agriculture. The appropriation of the government limited the work to the area infested by the boll weevil. A conference with Dr. F. T. Gates, Dr. Buttrick, and Dr. Knapp, and later with Secretary Wilson, of the Department of Agriculture, promptly removed this difficulty. Dr. Knapp was invited to Washington to take charge of the Farm Demonstration Work in the Department of Agriculture and the General Education Board supplied the funds necessary to carry it on in the Southern states, outside the weevil area. It was begun in Mississippi in 1906, in Alabama and

Virginia in 1907, and in 1908 it was extended into every Southern state. State, district, and county agents were appointed as rapidly as suitable persons could be found, and under the inspiration of Dr. Knapp they went about their work with all the zeal and unselfishness of a religious movement.

In the direction of the agents Dr. Knapp showed himself a great teacher. He would never permit them to undertake too much at one time. He was simply concerned that the farmer should begin where he was, no matter how far down that was, and take the first step forward. The next year there would be another and a longer stride and then the way was easy. In his homely wisdom he would say to the agents— "Don't confuse people with elaborate programs; the average man, like the crow, cannot count more than three."

Dr. Knapp was always eager to help the poor and disadvantaged farmer. He said, "The only way such farmers can prosper is by remaining in the old rut and improving the rut." Having taken the first step, he could take the next and end by diversified farming, but he knew the sheer folly of talking diversification to a man down and out, who had to borrow money on the one cash crop which the credit system, evil as it was, recognized. Seeing with an understanding eye the economic and social impediments, he was always quick with human sympathy, never merely critical, but always definite, simple, straightforward.

A cynic might say that Dr. Knapp drew upon the best agricultural knowledge already available and simply took it to the farmers—a simple enough task. Yes, it was so simple, we wonder why it wasn't done before. This is a commonplace remark about any invention or any step of social progress. But it was just here that Dr. Knapp made his great contribution, and his whole life was a preparation for it. He knew that poor farmers do not become good farmers by attending lectures or reading bulletins any more than a boy masters algebra by having a text-book available for his use on a library shelf. He stated his own method as follows: "The farmer must solve this problem on his own farm and with his own hands and find the answer in the crib or granary."

His method was the method of the Great Teacher who chose a few men who in turn went out and touched the lives of men in all parts of the world. The individual was never lost sight of. The agent visited the farmer and got him to agree to cultivate an acre of corn or cotton according to directions which would be furnished him. He then signed a contract with the U. S. Department of Agriculture. Carefully selected seed would be furnished, and the agent would visit the farmer once or twice a month. At the time of his visit some of the neighbors would be on hand to see how the demonstration was turning out and to get the agent's directions. The man would succeed and his success thrust him forward as a leading man. The seed from his project was in demand at a good price. He was ready to go on. He plied the agent with questions; he became a student of farm bulletins, an observer of farm practice, eager to learn. The neighbors would be ready to undertake the work, and so better practice would spread.

The full significance of the Demonstration Work cannot be appreciated unless we see it in perspective against the social and economic background of Southern life. In the foreword of his book, "South of Panama," Professor Ross sums up much of the history of Latin American countries in the sentence, "South America is the victim of a bad start." Lest we flatter ourselves because of our superior progress, he adds that the history of North America would have been very different had the first settlers found here a native population engaged in agriculture, patient and peaceable, ready to be exploited, such as the Spanish conquistadors found on the continent to the south.

Fortune favored us in selecting for our progenitors the adventurous, the daring, the lovers of hardship, those whose religious or political views placed them at a disadvantage in the old world, and who looked forward to a society ordered in accordance with their own standard of values. Some came, too, who had failed, social derelicts in the old world, but they had the will to make a fresh start and the new world put a premium upon industry and looked to the future rather than the past.

But the start was not all good. The institution of slavery slowly fastened itself as a blight upon the colonies. It was stoutly resisted by the freedom-loving middle class. It scarcely got a foothold in the Northern states, where it was never profitable, but in the South there was a conflict of interests. The large tobacco planters of Virginia, the rice and indigo planters of the Carolina coast, found it profitable and suited to the culture of these crops, so there grew up a class of wealthy land owners who held most of the slaves. The non-slaveholding whites, who would have found employment as skilled laborers and as small farmers, began to move westward to the frontier, to the mountains and beyond, and society began to take on the form of several distinct strata. Jefferson and other leaders of the Revolution cast all the weight of their influence against the spread of Negro slavery. They kept it out of the Northwest Territory, and in Virginia the movement for the abolition of slavery grew steadily until 1833 when Nat Turner's insurrec-

tion and the rise of the Abolitionists in the North
had the effect of solidifying local sentiment
against it. From that time on, criticism of "our
institutions" began to be looked upon as a mild
form of treason. The soft pedal was put upon
public utterances. Freedom of discussion waned
and practically vanished.

The invention of the cotton gin in 1793 stimulated the rapid settlement of the Southwest.
The new lands of Alabama, Mississippi, Louisiana, and Texas, were rapidly cleared and
brought under cultivation to supply the expanding market for the South's great product.
The same conflict of interests continued. The
white man with no capital but his own hardi-
hood and love of independence was always pushing to the frontier, ready to fight the Indians, to
drive back the Mexicans, and to set up for himself in a new country; but always the richer
planters with large numbers of slaves would get
possession of the choice lands for cotton and
sugar cane. Thus, the fertile belt of black
prairie soil running across Alabama into Mississippi soon became referred to as the black belt
because of the character of the population, as
well as of the soil. With new land more fertile
and cheap ever waiting to be cleared and brought
under the plow, it was inevitable that the older
plantations of the states to the east should lose
their fertility. Thus the clearing of land and

cultivating it without fertilization until it was
no longer profitable and then "turning it out"
to grow up in pine forests became a fixed custom
in Southern agriculture. It is still done in some
parts of the South today. As a boy I remember
seeing on the old farms in Virginia such pine
forests, showing the ridges of the rows of corn
and tobacco when the land was last cultivated.
I thought all of this sort of thing went back to
the time of the Civil War, but later I learned
differently. Frederick Law Olmsted saw the
same thing in 1853. In *A Journey in the Seaboard
Slave States*, he speaks of getting lost in riding
through forests with pines one hundred feet tall
on land that had once been under cultivation
in the vicinity of Petersburg, Virginia. Himself
a farmer in New York state, he interviewed a
great number of Southern farmers and after careful calculation concluded that slave labor was
more expensive than free labor, and he wondered
at the crude and clumsy implements with which
the slaves worked; but he was assured that nothing else would stand the abuse and neglect.

Population dwindled for many decades in
some of the older counties of the seaboard states.
There were two migrations, one of the planter
class with their slaves to the newer lands of the
Southwest, another of the small farmer to
Indiana, Illinois, Missouri, Kansas, and other
regions of the West. Some went to find better

opportunities for the planatation system; others to escape from an economic system which placed them at a disadvantage. The extent of the migration of the planter class is well known. There are many marks of it in the names of counties and towns in the Lower South. Slavery took a fresh hold, and the masterful men of that time knew that its continuance was contingent upon the opening up of new lands.

The reader is referred to Professor Turner's *The Rise of the New West,* and to Helper's *The Impending Crisis,* for a valuable discussion of the movement north and west from the old Southern states. Helper relates that a professor in the University of North Carolina was dismissed because of a public address, in which he referred to the thousands of young people who had migrated from North Carolina to the free states of the West in order to escape the evil effects of slavery, and expressed the hope that they would aid in making Kansas a free state. It is a far cry from the university of that day to the great institution at Chapel Hill today with its unhampered freedom of opinion and its eager, critical inquiry into all departments of life and thought in its supreme desire to serve the people of the state.

After the Civil War the plantation system continued, substituting tenant labor for slave labor. Old habits and customs were hard to

break. The defeated people cherished with
something of a halo the things of the old order.
The Negroes proved themselves loyal friends
and preferred to stay on in their old homes,
making a new start with their former masters.
But making a new start did not mean a change
of methods. Old habits could not suddenly be
thrown aside. The old wasteful practices went
on. Under the tenant system the local merchant
and the banker assumed a new importance.
They advanced food and supplies necessary
"to run" the tenant through the year and took
a crop lien. The risk being great, the interest
was correspondingly high. As long, however,
as owners could feel reasonably sure of a rent of
a certain number of bales of cotton from their
tenants, they made no effort to change the
system but were willing to help them borrow
over again each new year. Indeed, many planters
considered it necessary to keep a tenant in debt
as a safeguard against his moving away. Unfortunately, most of the small owners were caught
in the toils of the same system, as they had to
borrow money. Once in debt, it was a difficult
matter to escape.

Southern agriculture was therefore in a vicious
circle. The soil fertility was seriously depleted;
the economic system kept the farmer in debt
at a high rate of interest, and discouraged
diversification. Crops were produced with a

maximum of man power and a minimum of horse power and improved machinery. Poor schools and highways were the natural corollaries and added to the difficulty of change.

Dr. Knapp analyzed this situation with great clearness and he addressed himself to the remedy with so much intelligence, kindness, and simplicity that he became the beloved apostle to the Southern farmers. He had abounding faith in Southern agriculture. In his address at Pinehurst, North Carolina, in 1907, he made the following statement: "To me the Southern States surpass all of the countries of the earth of equal area in material resources, mainly undeveloped. Underneath almost every acre is concealed a mineral wealth of surpassing value; within almost every acre are agricultural resources that, touched by intellect and labor, will reveal marvelous products. To me the Southern people are the purest stock of the greatest race the world has produced. The rural population has lived under unfortunate conditions for the best development, but the essential material of their natures is not impaired and it requires but leadership to attain great results."

In characteristic vein he said of the credit system then in operation: "It submitted voluntary for involuntary servitude, ownership by agreement and poverty by contract under fear of the sheriff, for ownership by birthright and a government by proprietary right. So we have lived under a slavery where the chains are ingeniously forged and the bands riveted with gold. It is all the same in effect, the impoverishment of the masses."

He then set to work to get the farmers to improve the rut they were in, so that they could get out of it after two or three years; and he persuaded the bankers and merchants that their best interests lay in getting the farmer out of debt, making of him a depositor and a buyer of the comforts of life instead of the bare necessities. He soon had their cooperation. The response of the farmers was immediate, particularly among the middle class living on their own farms. The following example is typical.

A discouraged farmer in Alabama, already in debt $1,250.00, without a cow or hog of any kind, and with only a pair of old mules, was in danger of losing his home and 125 acres of land. The demonstration agent persuaded him to follow Dr. Knapp's instructions in the cultivation of a few acres each of corn and of cotton. He made a bale of cotton per acre, and 50 bushels of corn per acre on the demonstration plots, which was treble the yield under the old method. The following year he extended these methods to his entire farm with the same fortunate results. At the end of the second year he was out of debt, and had besides a new pair of mules,

three cows, $300.00 worth of hogs, 700 bushels
of corn, and $400.00 on deposit in bank. He
wrote a letter to Dr. Knapp, saying, "I can't
find words to express my appreciation of what
the Demonstration Work has done for me."

The following quotation from the field notes
of a demonstration agent in Georgia is an indication of the rapid progress among the demonstration farmers: "One man has cotton six to nine
inches high, with roots sixteen to twenty inches
long as the result of deep plowing in winter,
while his neighbors are replanting. I saw 12 pure-
bred Berkshire sows on vetch and rye pastures.
Farm implements doubled in one year in one
county as the result of farm tool demonstration
on the farm. Farmers have bought over 4,000
two-horse plows since last fall and are buying
harrows faster than men can supply them. Forty
cars of farm implements as against two last year
were sold by one wholesale dealer as the result
of demonstration talk. . . . There has been sold
in one county a car load of good western mares."

With such a response among the adult farmers,
Dr. Knapp recognized that the need for the
work among the grown-up farmers would dis-
appear, if the work could be carried on among
the boys. Accordingly, in 1908, boys' corn clubs
were organized and by 1913 over 90,000 boys
were enrolled. The best results were accomplished among boys. They were eager to learn

and on their mettle to excel their parents. The results were astonishing. "In 1910, for example, the boys' clubs of Holmes County, Mississippi, averaged 76 bushels of corn per acre, while their fathers were averaging 16. In the same season, 100 boys in various parts of the South averaged 133.7 bushels, and one boy produced over 200; the following season, 100 boys averaged 137.48 bushels, 7 boys raised over 200; in 1911, 471 made over 100 bushels to the acre; in 1912, 493."[1]

Two years later, in 1910, a further extension of the Demonstration Work was made in the organization of girls' canning and poultry clubs. This work grew out of some canning clubs organized in Aiken County, South Carolina, by Miss Marie Cromer, and a similar work in Virginia undertaken the same summer by Miss Ella G. Agnew. The girls first cultivated one-tenth of an acre in the home gardens, usually beginning with tomatoes. They met in each other's homes and under the direction of the agents canned the fruit and vegetables in the most approved and attractive manner. This work was later known as the Home Demonstration Work. The story of boys and girls who have become aroused by the Demonstration Work and who have graduated from local high schools and obtained a college education through their own earnings in these home projects, is one of the

[1] From Report of The General Education Board.

most inspiring chapters in the development of public education in the South. Jerry Moore, a fifteen year old boy in Florence County, South Carolina, made an unheard of yield on his acre—228 bushels of corn, and was awarded a scholarship to Clemson College. This yield was afterwards surpassed by Walker Lee Dunson, of Alabama, who made 232 7/10 bushels at a cost of 19 cents per bushel on his demonstration acre. A Sunday-school teacher was asking a class of boys about the prophets in the Old Testament. "No," said a little boy, "I don't know anything about Jeremiah, but I can tell you all about Jerry Moore and his big corn crop."

Some of the most interesting stories of the Demonstration Work have to do with Negro farmers, for two Negro agents, Mr. John B. Pierce of Virginia, and Mr. T. M. Campbell, of Tuskegee, Alabama, were appointed by Dr. Knapp and the number has steadily increased. I frequently visited demonstration farmers who worked under Mr. Pierce's direction. I recall several in Nottoway County, Virginia. Daniel Tucker made 65 bushels of corn on his demonstration acre, whereas the yield on the same kind of land on the rest of his place was only 24 bushels to the acre. The demonstration acre, in addition to the corn, had a crop of cowpeas planted at the last working to restore fertility and humus to the soil. The next farmer, William

Keeton, proudly showed us his corn, his hay, and his hogs, and other livestock. He had food and feed enough for his own use, and his tobacco crop was a real cash crop. He was no longer in debt and he had just finished remodeling his dwelling-house. The next farmer, William Jones, was a very old man, who had had a hard struggle paying for a little land and just making a bare living for himself and his family. After two years of demonstration farming, he had built a new home, a neat, well furnished cottage, and the old home was being used as a kitchen. It was like a benediction to hear the old man tell of the transformation that had come through the visit of the demonstration agent and how he hoped that all of his people might learn these lessons in their youth.

A new schoolhouse, in charge of a Hampton graduate, replacing an old log building, a neatly painted church with services every Sunday, and the testimony of the leading banker that the colored people were saving money and taking a new pride in their homes, completed the story of the transformation of this colored community.

Another interesting story is told by a demonstration agent on St. Helena Island, off the coast of South Carolina. The Negro farmers on the Island considered 15 bushels of corn per acre a good yield. They were very suspicious of anything new and the demonstration agent could persuade the first year only six farmers to grow an acre of corn under the demonstration methods. These six made two or three times as much corn as they had ever made before, and one, Rev. D. C. Washington, made over 50 bushels on his acre. When he got his 50-bushel button from the U. S. Department of Agriculture, he wore it proudly on his coat, and the following Sunday preached an impressive sermon on "Opening the eyes of the blind." He said that he had been farming in blindness for thirty years, but the Demonstration Work had opened his eyes, and now he could not only see how to raise corn, but a great light of hope had come into his life for all the people on the Island.

With the passage of the Smith-Lever Act in 1914, Demonstration Work was made national in scope and became a regular part of the extension work of the State Agricultural Colleges with substantial sums appropriated by the federal government. The Smith-Hughes Act in 1917 carried the plan still further in providing federal aid for teachers of vocational agriculture and home economics in rural high schools. Under this plan boys and girls 14 years of age may undertake projects at their homes under the direction of the teacher. They keep accurate records and have whatever profit or bear whatever loss is incurred in the projects they undertake. This work, like the boys' corn clubs, has stimulated thousands of country boys to stay in school, remain on the farm, and become successful farmers.

Dr. Knapp did not live to see the work completely taken over by the federal and state governments. He died in Washington, April 1, 1911, but he lived to see his best hopes realized. The work was already successfully organized for the farmers, for the boys, for the girls and their mothers, and it was rapidly extending to all parts of the South. The Demonstration Work had moved the entire South as no other movement had ever done. Every demonstration farm was like a little leaven, from which helpful ideas were spreading. The people took on new confidence and hope. The period of the Demonstration Work from 1906 to 1914, was precisely the period of the most rapid development in public education. The Demonstration Work was in effect a spiritual movement. Every man that had been helped by the agent invariably wanted to help his neighbors. He felt a community consciousness, and a new pride in the church, the schoolhouse, the public roads. New laws were enacted, obstructive sections of state constitutions were removed by amendments, local taxation for school purposes developed. The old one-teacher schools were being replaced by consolidated schools, and the establishment of rural high schools went on at an amazing pace. Not only was an enormous amount of rural wealth created, but spiritual forces were also released, as wealth became invested more and more in schools, churches, highways, public health, and all other agencies of public welfare. This was a long step towards the realization of Dr. Knapp's own vision, as he expressed it in an address before the Conference for Education in the South, at Pinehurst, North Carolina, in 1907.

"Let it be the high privilege of this great and free people to establish a republic where rural pride is equal to civic pride, where men of the most refined taste and culture select the rural villa, and where the wealth that comes from the soil finds its greatest return in developing and perfecting that great domain of nature which God has given to us as an everlasting estate."

Dr. Knapp always strove for a self-sustaining system of agriculture. He showed the folly of raising cotton or tobacco merely to pay for corn, hay and pork, which could be raised in the South more cheaply than in the West. Thus Louisiana, was buying corn in 1908, but by 1911 the farmers of that state produced a surplus beyond their own needs. In the same way livestock and dairying became well established in various parts of the cotton states. Cooperative packing houses for the curing of pork have been established in various centers, and several of the large Chicago packers have established branch plants

in these states, in order to handle the increasing
output of hogs and cattle from Southern farmers.
For example, the corn crop of Alabama has
increased from 35,053,000 bushels in 1900 to
48,988,000 bushels in 1923. In the same period
the hay crop increased from 85,000 to 636,000
tons and the value of livestock from $18,000,000
to $90,000,000.

It is impossible to estimate the importance
of this work in preparing the Southern states
for the crisis of the World War. Not only were
their own needs supplied, but a large surplus
of foodstuff was produced to meet the demands
of Europe. Dr. Knapp had worked out a procedure which the government promptly extended on a national scale, thereby greatly
increasing food production and releasing trans-
portation equipment needed for war supplies.

With the cutting off of much of the European
market for cotton coincident with the very large
crop in 1914, Southern farmers felt the pinch of
hard times, but with the high prices that
followed, they enjoyed an unprecedented prosperity. In 1920 North Carolina ranked fourth
among all the states in the Union in the value of
farm products, aggregating $683,168,000, and
Georgia was just a lap behind with a total crop
value of $613,240,000.

The next crisis in Southern agriculture came
with the falling prices and general deflation,

but instead of following wild schemes of relief or attempting to apply political remedies, farmers soberly went about the task of forming coöperative marketing associations. The tobacco growers of Kentucky, Virginia and the Carolinas have nearly 200,000 farmers in their associations. Prices are being stabilized and the farmers are facing the future, confident of their ability to handle their own business in the changing markets of the world. Similar movements are under way for cotton, peanuts and other staple crops. This is but one of the several lateral developments of the Demonstration Work. The primary object of the Demonstration Work was to increase production. Having greatly increased production through skill, intelligence, superior equipment and machinery, the next step is being taken through these coöperative associations for a better system of distribution, which will stabilize the markets and bring the business of agriculture to a parity with other big business of the twentieth century.

AUGUSTUS BALDWIN LONGSTREET
A Southern Cultural Type

BY

JOHN DONALD WADE

AUGUSTUS BALDWIN LONGSTREET

A certain lady long ago wrote a cook-book that attained wide popularity throughout the South. Canny person that she was, this author was rich in her suggestions of alternatives. "Use," she would say, "the juice of three lemons —or, if lemons are not at hand, vinegar may be substituted."

It is a puzzle to find out how often a good Georgian in mixing the patrio-historic dressing for his life is bound to resort to second choices. What magnificent rich cherry is there which he can impress for garnishment, what quite inimitable sprig of parsley, what watercress? We have Alexander Stephens to show, and we have Lanier. The disposition is strong to acclaim others; if one garnishment is not at hand, why, then—

Then Longstreet. He was of us, for us, with us. To name the impulses that bore him on, and to trace his stout, at last unavailing resistance to those impulses imply the blocking out of a sketch that one would swear inconsequential did not the hasty lines of it inevitably keep falling into shapes that are tragic and even noble. Tragic, chiefly because he was brave; noble, chiefly because he was true. Bravery he manifested in common with the pioneer nation to which he belonged; truth he manifested most strikingly apart from it.

The dominion of candor is apparently not yet established anywhere in this world. In the United States, and particularly in the South, its claims upon human allegiance seem rather less strong than they do elsewhere. It is safe to say that our condition did not occultly rise up out of hell to stifle us; it developed from many great and slight causes. Some of these are cosmic in import and need not be discussed; but it is as well in passing to single out at least one of them, perhaps the chief, namely, the wicked and deceitful heart of man. That, we can hardly at this time, very comfortably put from us.

There are some other considerations, however, which can be pretty definitely isolated and examined. One of them is the Puritan's refusal to attach importance to any craving that has its origin in the senses. Another is the pioneer's refusal to admit the existence of anything which might discourage immigration. Still another, more evident in the post-bellum South than elsewhere, is the instinctive refusal of any man to throw a burden of unfavorable opinions upon a fellow creature already struggling for life.

What, in principle, would have been the judgment of, say, Cotton Mather, upon the importance of substituting vinegar for lemon juice?

He would probably have thought the whole matter too trivial for his attention, but if compelled to say just why it was too trivial, he would have reasoned this way: it is all an affair of sensuous enjoyment, and concern about it would only take up time that ought to be spent pondering eternal mysteries. Now most pioneer Americans were largely brought up on Mather's own catechism. They feared God quite as much as he did.

And they loved man and what man makes somewhat more than he did. These American forests were lonesome and dangerous; and there was much sentiment in early times (as there is in Miami and Los Angeles in these times) toward going any length to further pleasant report of the new lands, in districts naturally looked upon as reservoirs of population and wealth.

Governor John Winthrop in his history of New England gives the edifying story of some caitiffs who in 1642 abandoned Massachusetts and returned to England. On their voyage they spoke reproachfully of the people and the country they had left. Straightway storms broke upon them. "Then they humbled themselves before the Lord, and acknowledged God's hand to be justly out against them. Only one of them had not joined the rest, but spake well of the people and of the country; upon this, it pleased the Lord to spare their lives. Yet the Lord followed them on shore. One had a daughter

that presently ran mad. Another, a school-
master, had no sooner hired an house, and gotten
in some scholars, but the plague set in and took
away two of his children.''

Bad "religion," then, to indulge oneself in
changes that would gratify only temporal demands; bad "patriotism" to admit publicly that
all is not precisely as it should be. In both of
these matters Longstreet was fortunate. In
"religion," he was sketpical, and in "patriotism,"
too devoted to believe that his country needed
prescriptive adulation. He was inherently frank,
and he was endowed with the perspective that
came of a long residence away from home. He
was also fortunate in that his principal activities
began just at the moment when Georgia at large
was most buoyantly self-confident—long enough
after the state had obviously got under way for
a prosperous voyage, long enough before the seas
had been made choppy by the unwearied sus-
pirations of the abolitionists.

As a boy about Augusta, Longstreet was
aggressive in everything except intellectual attainment, but when he was about seventeen
years old he came under the influence of a young
fellow named George McDuffie, a sort of intellectual prodigy who was so amiable that Longstreet
decided to be as nearly like him as possible.
That decision necessitated a brand of education
different from any he had yet known.

It was generally conceded that the Reverend Doctor Moses Waddel, who was then conducting a back-woods school some miles above Augusta, could give out learning according to unique and effective methods. With contagious enthusiasm he aimed to apply reason starkly, to life as well as to education, but he did not stint the perverse humor of his mind which was always showing him how absurdly, on occasion, his program might work out.

Longstreet became a student at this school; and he was influenced there, profoundly, by Waddel himself, and by the numerous promising young men with whom he formed friendships. But most of all, he was influenced by John C. Calhoun, Doctor Waddel's brother-in-law, then just back from his educational ventures in New England. He, too, seemed to Longstreet the very pink of amiability, worthier of imitation, perhaps, than McDuffie.

Calhoun had been a student at Yale, and later, in Litchfield, Connecticut, at a law school which was then the best of its kind in this country. Longstreet followed him. After about two years at each place he returned to Georgia, and when he was twenty-five years old entered upon the practice of law. This was in 1815.

Two years more, and Longstreet removed from Augusta to Greensboro, a village about seventy-five miles away toward the now rapidly retreating frontier. His parents had followed this movement from New Jersey to Georgia and it was natural that he, in turn, should follow it also; but it is likely that the definite cause of his going to Greensboro was his marriage to a young woman of that place.

Frances Eliza Parke was eighteen years old, an heiress in her own right; and one of the items of her wealth was about thirty slaves. Longstreet's marriage with her did two things for him. It enmeshed him in the blissful coils of a domesticity that at last wrested—or allured as to brighter worlds—his naturally free-thinking religious impulses into the most conforming orthodoxy. It also involved him straightway, rich man now that he was, in the almost equally blissful coils of an economic order which, everywhere more and more assailed from without, was beginning to demand of its votaries a compliance more and more absolute.

Before he was led away from himself into the castle of respectable formalism, then still in the building, he struggled so manfully that one finds it hard ever to leave off loving him. And indeed throughout his life, as a sort of royal prisoner, he was always, from time to time, uttering whoops of derisive laughter or mirthful sympathy that must have seemed very unmannerly to his house-mates.

Fannie Parke's father and mother found themselves captivated by their new son-in-law. And everybody else was captivated. The young man was extremely well informed, and his manners were ingratiating. He was garrulous and given to much joking, distinctive, but not too conspicuously an original to be respectable. He believed that the American Revolution was the crowning event of all history, and he felt himself, in his simple capacity of American citizen, "standing above the rest of the world on a lofty peak of moral elevation." Such sentiments were popular.

Now it is obviously not a stimulant to effort to consider oneself thus far superior to one's fellows, but Longstreet was above everything companionable—not only, in actuality, with his neighbors, but, in fancy, with any living creature his imagination might confront him with. It seems sure that he indulged himself in his vision of superiority more fully when he was mounted on some rostrum for campaign purposes, than he did while he was whittling out picture frames, or grafting his apple trees, or pottering away with his silk worms, or conducting his little loan business.

Lofty patriotic sentiment, it is true, he probably reserved most generally for lofty rostrums, but patriotic utterances, nevertheless, played

their sure part in sending him to the state legislature in 1821, and in procuring for him a year
later a position as Judge of the Superior Court.
In 1824, he became a candidate for election to
the national congress, and every chance seemed
moving as he would have it.

Then, in the midst of his campaign, he suffered
the death of his little son, Alfred. He withdrew
from the race and entered upon a religious inquiry, which resulted most satisfactorily. He
had been a skeptic; within a fortnight, he says,
all his doubts vanished. Within three years he
became a member of the Methodist Church;
within ten years more, a minister.

But Longstreet found trouble in being anything unreservedly. The Methodists of his time
were cold to sensuous appeal, deaf to many
claims to virtue advanced by people whose
religious dogma (it was reported) did not coin-
cide with the dogma which (it was reported)
was the lodestar of Methodism. The new convert
had heard much argument about it up to his
thirty-eighth year, before he capitulated, and he
was not so easily to give over the rigidness of
his convictions. There were some points he
preferred about the Methodists, and some others
about the Baptists. He said so. As for the con-
ventional animosity he ought to feel for the
Baptist denomination, he simply could not rise
to it—he had wandered too long in darkness

ever quite to get the knack of things. For the life of him he could never understand why if a Catholic prayed a good prayer it was improper for him to chime in with Amen—he went that far.

As for asceticism, he wondered how a thing so rarely practiced could be so generally preached. "I cannot," he says, "think that the interest of religion is served by cutting off any one innocent enjoyment." Dangerous talk that, from a temperance agitator, particularly from one who would not himself become a "teetotaler."

Longstreet lived in Greensboro ten years before again taking up his residence in Augusta. Those ten years, and what he learned in them, their friendliness and informality of intercourse, their slapdash versatility of attainment, their disposition to revere standard virtues—and neglect other virtues—these forever thereafter created the Judge's unique spiritual stock-in-trade. They are attributes that do not lose their freshness if they are properly cured; and frankness is among the best of all salts.

To many people it is not a tasteful salt; but a mature man who has truth clamoring in his heart cannot hold his counsel always out of regard for popular sensibilities.

During the early 1830's, Longstreet set forth, in a series of half-actual half-fictitious newspaper sketches, his observations on the social development of Georgia. They are kindly and humorous, but they do not gloss over any defects, nor do they weaken their indictment with any confession of burlesque—on the contrary, the author states explicitly that they are not burlesque. No one could tell how they would be received. They were printed anonymously, but the secret of their authorship soon transpired, and Longstreet was generously praised everywhere. He had kept off the subjects that important people are traceably connected with, and everyone was able to think that the sketches had reference to his neighbors rather than to himself. They were excessively popular throughout the United States up to the period of the Civil War; and to the present, under their collective title, Georgia Scenes, they retain significance as one of the earliest examples of American realism.

People are willing enough to accept social comment made under a veil of humor, but the more direct type of criticism that finds itself nagging the world toward exertion is less welcome. When Longstreet began nagging, his contemporaries soon found instinctively what to do with him; they put him at the head of a boys' school where nagging is held salutary, and where it cannot be resented. Their liberality in tolerating him even in that fastness was remarkable. It was due somewhat, of course, to the fact that he had become a preacher—and preachers are supposed to quarrel—but it was due more largely to the fact that the evils he named were then too patently in way of remedying themselves to need either denial or justification. A little earlier, or a little later, this could not have been the case.

But Longstreet was not so easily shut up. He had some very definite suggestions as yet to make about politics.

Nationally, he thought Georgia should adopt Nullification. His advice was disregarded, and he divulged his opinion that a good many states would probably surprise some people before long by withdrawing from the then existing Union and associating themselves with a Union formed about Texas as a nucleus. They would, in short, go west.

Locally, politics did not suit him much better. The idealism he once observed, or thought he observed, was somewhat absent. He was in position to see the corrupt courses of government and he thought it incumbent on him to speak his knowledge. The way to be elected to office in Georgia, he says, is to "treat liberally, ape dignity here, crack obscene jokes there, sing vulgar songs in one place, talk gravely in another." And the legislature, filled with mountebanks and demagogues, "has enacted measures which for extravagance and folly have no parallel in the codes of enlightened nations." For

Longstreet's part, he was independent. He held it the "bounden duty of a candidate openly to avow his sentiments, particularly those which are averse to the prevailing opinion of those to whom he offers himself." It is hardly necessary to set down the result of his various candidacies.

Logic left him only one retort: the people were not fit to govern themselves, anyhow. Whither, then, might they look for guidance? Hardly to any crown-heads; hardly to Judge Longstreet; perhaps, then, to God.

When Longstreet was a little boy in Augusta his father took him to a show at which, it developed, one of the actors was so presumptuous as to make Mr. Longstreet, Sr., the subject of a facetious ballad. The gentleman withdrew from the theater in great heat; the fresh air outside was more to his liking. The son never forgot that magnificent method of rebuke.

The political theater of Georgia in the late 1830's was ribald, and the man who as a little boy had once seen his father withdraw so effectively, now began picturing himself as outside this house altogether, bathed in the fresh air of moral and mystical speculation. "Human laws and governments," he wrote, "have ever failed and ever must fail of their ends. The Christian religion would supersede them all."

In accord, then, with youthful memories, as well as with pioneer instinct, whenever one

place grew insupportable, Longstreet moved on
to another. He became a minister of the Methodist Church in 1838. Entering a new realm,
he carried over with him no contrivances to mol-
lify the buffetings he might encounter. A plague
fell upon the city of Augusta, but he remained
there, faithful to the nicest whispers of his conscience, exposing himself to the disease un-
guardedly whenever he could make himself use-
ful.

A year later, at nearly fifty, he accepted the
presidency of Emory College, a Methodist institution only a few months in operation. Here,
as his wont had been, the Judge was frank and
adventurous, and by consequence, at times
quarrelsome. But youth is very tolerant of
frankness and venturesomeness—more tolerant
than age, with its accumulation of secret mis-
deeds and its stiff joints, can well afford to be—
and it was accordingly in his contact with young-
sters that Longstreet did the best work of his
life. If a policy of his, helpful in that it restrained
his students, at times restrained him also in its
operation, he stood to his position and bore his
punishment. This engaging procedure, so rarely
observed among mature persons, seemed to the
bizarre judgment of youth, not folly, but very
worshipful honesty. And he had a way of
thought comprehensible to people who have yet
before them some fifty or sixty years in which

to accomplish things. "Merit, like water," he told his students, "will find its level, though it may have to wind through many a loaming vale, and leap many a rugged precipice before it does so."

The President further won the regard of his students by his attitude toward the important matter of enjoying oneself. Hard to please as he was, he seldom talked of what is forbidden— those things he made clear by example, his way of living. As for precept—through that, one heard chiefly of bright virtues to which any true man might lift up his heart passionately.

With what eager pride his following of boys must have gabbled over the long debate, between their idol and another minister, with reference to the iniquity of employing instrumental music in divine services. Longstreet thought music would really help, and he said so, earnestly, vigorously, but with unvarying dignity. His opponent was so violent, so ranting, that only a very spiritless young fellow could have witnessed the fray without having his sympathies stirred in behalf of a fighter who was too brave to adopt the barbarous tactics of his adversary.

But not students only, admired Longstreet's course at the General Conference of the Methodist Church held in 1844. Even the numerous good Southerners who had always thought him

dangerous were bound after that event to consider him a benefactor.   Amid the rasp and
bickering of that obscene week, Longstreet stood
cool and helpful and conciliatory.   But patience
has its limits.   At last, he decided, with his bloc,
that the free air of the slave-owning South was
more to his liking than any air contaminated
with Northern breathings could be, ever.   And
from the theater of that Conference he withdrew
in great heat.

So was the Methodist church—representing
the phase of American life which is spiritual—
divided, its parts alienated (certainly for as long
as eighty years) over an issue which later (for
only four years) entered wedge-fashion into the
phase of American life which is political.   But
this rather indecent contrast would not have
been embarrassing to Longstreet.   In effect, the
Northern delegates at that Conference had sung
mocking ballads about causes that were sacred
to him—primarily about the conscientiousness
of Bishop Andrew, his neighbor and dear friend,
and for his part, he was through with those
delegates quite permanently.   He became one of
the most violent of all separatists; he doubted
whether there was a good Methodist in the entire
North.

In 1848 the President of Emory College in
Georgia became for a few months the President
of Centenary College in Louisiana.   And then

for several years he was President of the University of Mississippi. On any map those places
are both west of Georgia, and that alone gave
them some fascination in Longstreet's mind.
Before entering the ministry he had long been
haunted with an idea that if he could only move
west he could speedily get rich. And on Longstreet's map, at least, the business of being head
of a state school lay somewhat west of the
business of being head of a church school. Who
was he, by a wilful fixity, to be hindering, perhaps thwarting, the Course of Empire? And
beside, there was the consideration of a wider
field of usefulness—of course, there was that.

In Mississippi, it was held that to manifest
an interest in politics is incompatible with the
ideally cloistered life of a scholar. To get Longstreet into a cloister, however, was more than all
the trustees and all their horses could accomplish. He saw the Know Nothing Party becoming powerful, and he believed it a great menace.
It seemed to him cowardly and false, utterly
divorced from any good. Trustees might tug
till they grew tired. He would denounce cowardice and falsehood so long as he had breath,
God helping him. If they tugged to the extent
of annoying him, he threatened to resign, and
they desisted. He had saved the school from
ruin and made it powerful, and it was good
tactics to retain him. Once, however, they went

too far, and the old man in exasperation executed his threat, withdrawing shortly afterwards to a nearby farm on which he hoped to end his days, peacefully.

In little over a year he was in South Carolina, President of the State College at Columbia. Know Nothings had ceased from troubling him, but his unwearied spirit had found rest altogether intolerable. He was only sixty-eight, and Yankee abolitionists were menacing the peace of this continent. Their policy seemed to him cowardly and false, utterly divorced from any good. He would denounce cowardice and falsehood so long as—and so forth. Trustees we have with us always. There was one at hand to remonstrate—it happened a personal friend of old standing. Letters were exchanged. The one from the President stated that the writer loved his correspondent dearly, and was always interested to learn the opinions of a friend; the suggestions of a trustee, however, regarding a matter of non-official conduct—were these not a little intrusive? But more people, doubtless, than one lone trustee considered the old man outside his bounds.

There were troubles also within the college. The discipline of the institution had so declined that it could be restored only by very drastic measures. On that score, too, there was complaint. It was whispered that the president was not vitally interested in his classes. Damocles remembered his magic formula, and busied himself whetting a resignation, but before he could hoist it, new circumstances turned dissent into a din of acclamation.

He had had such luck before this. The acclaim this time had its genesis in London. Longstreet was there in 1860 as the representative of the United States at a gathering of scientists—it was a politician, one should state, who appointed him, not by any means the Lord God, not even Agassiz. When the scientists were assembled, a negro was introduced to them, and they were indiscreet enough to cheer. Longstreet simply would not abide it; in the grandest possible manner he stalked out of that convention. Cautious and sensible trustees thenceforth might reason as they would, but their reasoning had best be done inside their own heads, and kept there. President Longstreet was canonized; he was a grand old man, and Yankees and upstart niggers were equally despicable, and there was little chance of holding off a war anyway.

Little chance? Little wish to hold it off.

Then it comes, explosive, crashing, insatiate. The world tumbles in before it, and old Longstreet, set off frantically, goes hurtling round, catching vainly at all manner of things which suddenly turn as unstable as himself. Hold it off? He would give his life to hold it off. Who

dreamed the disagreement would come to this?
Who dreamed it? For the South to be fighting
the North, that truly was an occurrence greatly
to be deprecated, but for young John Heyward
to be going out to let some wretches shoot the
life out of him, for young George Rhett to be
going—(how that boy will keep reminding one,
somehow, of little Alfred Longstreet, dead now
these forty years!)—did one dream these boys
would be so foolish? South and North, all right;
but John Heyward and George Rhett—No!
No! No! We know what the hysteria came to.
John Heyward knew, also, before the year was
out; and George Rhett, likewise. And others
knew.

Once Longstreet recognized the war was inevitable, he furthered his section's cause in every
way at his command. His nephew, James Longstreet, and his son-in-law, L. Q. C. Lamar, were
figures of great prominence in the struggle, and
he himself was throughout the long four years
associated with the most important functionaries
conceivable. He ranged over the country from
South Carolina to Mississippi, and in spirit he
ranged the whole earth and all past time seeking
everywhere some sure swift stratagem whereby
he could foil the wicked power of the oppressor.
His activity was unbounded. Letters to Lamar,
letters to nephew James, manifestoes to the
Southern Armies, went from him constantly.

He was busy, too, with the social obligations which naturally devolve upon a distinguished man who unremittingly chooses distinguished people for his hosts. And he was busy preaching to the soldiers, busy mistrusting President Davis, busy wishing General Lee would use his spade less and his gun more, busy teaching arithmetic to little white and negro children, busy praying God, fervently, fervently, not to hear the prayers ascending to Him daily in behalf of Grant.

Then Appomattox. His dear South lay quite broken. It was as if at the end of some dark foreboding he had come upon the mangled body of a sweet child, a delicate girl, whom he had loved with utmost tenderness. Life was so flat to him. Every syllable of reprimand that he had ever spoken to her rose to his mind to sear it. O God, if you will spare her, spare her, never, never while I live will I say aught to her except in way of praise!

And every neighbor of his, every friend, was bowed in equal grief. Never, never against the names of people who had suffered so unjustly could he again let his swift mind enregister one fault. He could only love them, and, on Sundays, preach to them of bright Heaven and its joys of reunited love, sing to them, upon occasion, in the course of his sermons, hymns whose rolling cadences seemed at times to bear them all up wellnigh against the gleaming ramparts of Paradise.

But at last that stricken child regains her strength, and certain people, remembering her past hoydenish enterprises, think it well to shake a finger, and say that recklessness and folly may always expect an overthrow. But to Longstreet and his kind, the barest hint of blame is heinous sacrilege. At all costs, that kind of talk must be silenced forthwith, conclusively. That, then, was a thing to live for. And so the old weary processes, re-exhilarated by the wine of a new aim, begin afresh.

Books to read, vindications to establish, invectives to hurl, Bible manuscripts to translate, grandchildren to teach the art of flute-playing, land records to make unmistakable, God, always, to be prayed to. How the days go!

One morning a friend saw him grafting apple-twigs. "Judge," he inquired, "do you ever expect to eat any apples off that twig?" "No," the old man answered, "but someone else will."

Soon now, he knew well, he would be moving on. What of it? Across the world he had left his trail of apple trees—in Augusta, in Greensboro, around Emory College, in Louisiana, in Mississippi. Always he had planted in full knowledge that he might reap no benefit—so shifting a world it is—but he had never therefore planted the less faithfully. . . . It is a trait to be very glad over.

* * *

In the summer of 1870, the old transient
cleared out, definitely, his face beaming as with
a vision, his lips—obeying the dictate of a still
resilient mind—calling aloud, "Look! Look!"
What fine new country a little west, there, did
those eyes behold?

JOEL CHANDLER HARRIS

Constructive Realist

BY

JULIA COLLIER HARRIS

JOEL CHANDLER HARRIS

Long before his death in 1908 Joel Chandler Harris was known to the world as the author of the "Uncle Remus" stories—literally to all the world of fiction readers, for these beguiling negro myths made such an appeal that they were translated into many languages. I have a copy done into the Bengali dialect by an English missionary and illustrated by a native artist, and there is a version, also by a missionary, in one of the African dialects. The author received letters about the "Tar-Baby" story from all parts of the civilized world; learned professors in France, Germany, Austria, and England wrote to him concerning its origin; and reference to Br'er Rabbit's cuteness in this particular dilemma is so frequent and so general that the tale has come to rank with some of Æsop's and La Fontaine's in the realm of classic lore.

The universal popularity of the "Uncle Remus" tales is one of the gratifying episodes in American literature. That thousands of readers in many quarters have recognized the artistry of these tales, and have gotten from them the pure joy that only something completely human can give, is a hopeful symptom and halts the cynical critic in his inclination to label the "average reader" either a moron or a sensation seeker.

However the drop of gall always taints the honey-pot, and it is an undeniable paradox that the never-waning popularity of "Uncle Remus" has wrought a real injury to our literature, in that the other work of Joel Chandler Harris has been almost lost sight of through the determination of his admirers to cling exclusively to the animal fables so engagingly recounted by the old negro. Comparatively few people know that the author of "Uncle Remus" recorded with literary skill, inimitable humor and shrewd insight a phase of old-time Georgia life in rural communities in his "Sister Jane," "Gabriel Tolliver," "The Bishop and the Boogerman," "Mingo" "Free Joe," "Balaam and his Master" and other collections of short stories, some of which are now out of print. This is a real misfortune, since these chronicles of slavery days and reconstruction days are not only rich in vivid and truthful characterization, but are valuable historically in their faithful delineation of a phase of Southern life that has passed away.

Many of these stories are a vehicle for the author's philosophy and reveal qualities of mind and heart which place him in that small band of "moderns" whose vision and universality lift them out of the provincial and make them leaders in the best sense. It would be well if this side of the genius and character of Joel Chandler Harris could be brought to the knowledge of our young poeple, since the love of justice, the social sympathy, the spirit of good will, the hatred of shams which were at the foundation of his character and which are expressed in the work just referred to, as well as in his essays and editorials, offer the most effectual antidote to many of the glaring faults of our political and social life.

The facts of his youth are well known. A good deal of space was given them in my biography because I felt that his outlook on life and the trend of his literary work were immensely influenced by them. I need not enlarge on them here except to recall that he had to assume responsibility when other boys of his age were still frolicking in the fields and on the streets of the little Georgia town where he was born. Joel's mother, a woman of excellent family, had been deserted by his father before the boy's birth, but Mary Harris's strong nature and independent soul refused to sink under a misfortune which, in those days, was somewhat in the nature of a disgrace. Joel learned early the hard lessons of poverty and the developing lesson of work, and his mother, whose education and taste were good, made a practice of reading to him from the classics when the day's work was done.

In his early 'teens, Joel was befriended by a man of learning and influence, Joseph Addison

Turner, on whose plantation, near Eatonton, he
learned to be a printer, and in whose library,
a well-stocked one, he got the best part of his
education. He always insisted that Providence
overlooked him at every crisis of his life, and to
the devout this would doubtless seem plausible.
Certainly, wise and helpful friends lent him a
hand at critical moments, no doubt attracted
by his personality, which in his youthful days
must have been an artless compound of serious-
ness and whimsicality, of modesty and independence. His sensitive, upright nature could have
had no better sustenance than that which circumstances offered him. The discipline of responsibility made him thoughtful; the generous
kindness of influential friends toward him and
his mother made him merciful; the stigma of his
father's desertion made him keenly sympathetic
toward the misfortunes of others; the democratic
atmosphere of the little Georgia town made him
proof against snobbishness; his daily reading
among the best of the world's books safe-
guarded him against provincialism.

In a recent study of the literature of the old
South entitled "The Southern Plantation," Dr.
Francis P. Gaines makes the following comment
on the contribution of Joel Chandler Harris to
that body of writing:

"The popularity of the cycle of story-tellers,
Uncle Remus, Daddy Jake, Aunt Minervy Ann

and the others, has somewhat obscured a fact that is of supreme importance. This fact, which cannot be stated too emphatically, is that in Harris the whole plantation appears, not with the glamor of Page, but with a completeness of understanding not equalled by any other writer. Harris knew the plantation from one end to the other, and in his several stories, has reconstructed for us, bit by bit, the entire institution. With a sweeping inclusiveness running from the very structure of society, from the great problematic aspects, down to the single lovable personality, Harris's work is the literary history of the plantation."

Dr. Gaines shows critical discernment in thus noting that Joel Chandler Harris's manner of presentation of plantation life (and he might as truthfully have added of the life of rural Georgia communities after the Civil War) was that of a realist in the most accurate sense. He never let the glamorous memory of happy days on the Turner plantation, when his work in the printing-shop was enlivened by runs with the bird-dogs, or by hours of wonderful interest in the negro cabins, blind him to the darker aspects of slavery, such as the sufferings of fugitives, the tragedy of mixed blood, the separation of families or the occasional cruelties of overseers, and in this respect he differed from most of the Southern writers who distinguished themselves in the same field.

To be impressed with the author's sympathy toward those humble souls whose ignorance only heightens their tragedy, one has only to recall the pathos of Free Joe's vigils in the woods, night after night, in the hopes that his wife, who had been sold to the owner of a distant plantation, might be returned to him. Again, in "Blue Dave" we have a hint of the pitiful lot of the fugitive slave, and this subject is also treated in the account of the pursuit of Mink in "On the Plantation." The hopeless tragedy of mixed blood is considered in "The Case of Mary Ellen" and in a manner that is freighted with a sense of man's responsibility to his fellow-man, no matter of what color. "Where's Duncan" is the author's most poignant presentation of this species of injustice and its flavor of enigmatic terror reveals a side of the writer's genius which is nowhere else fully developed. "Mingo" is chiefly concerned with the havoc which is wrought upon the nature of the "poor white" by the arrogance and contempt of the aristocrat. The uncouth traits of the "poor white" woman, Feratia Bivins, who has been treated with injustice and scorn by the head of a great family, are depicted in sure and subtle fashion, and the story culminates in a burst of elemental rage and hatred on the part of the despised woman which tears to tatters the veil of sentimentality so often draped around the romantic figures of those who inhabit the "Big House."

These brief references to some of his short stories may indicate how modern and detached was his vision in depicting the "old regime" with its mansions, slave quarters, and "poor white" settlements. Though an optimist by nature, he observed with clear, just eyes and was as far from being deceived by any kind of "bunk" as his own Mr. Billy Saunders, the plain-spoken country-man, who later on became the author's mouth-piece in his editorials in *The Uncle Remus Magazine*. It is this clear-sightedness, together with a sense of humor akin to the soil in the same way as Bret Harte's or Mark Twain's, which gives these studies of life in middle Georgia fifty years ago a special value, and all who are familiar with them must have been impressed by their vivid character delineation, a quality which bespeaks a close acquaintance with the mental reactions of the types depicted. A hint of the author's method comes out in the following remarks to a young writer who applied to him some time in 1882 for advice about material for fiction:

"Permit me to suggest something about people with whom you are perfectly familiar," said the older writer. "It is a great step toward success when a young writer gains his or her consent to treat of things with which he or she is familiar.

It is worth while to remember that what is really great in literature is the *Commonplace*. Shakespeare is commonplace from beginning to end, and so is Thackeray. Did you ever notice the terrible meaning Mrs. Browning gives commonplace thoughts?"

In a letter to his son in 1890, when the latter was a schoolboy in Canada, he made a similar suggestion:

"You have a very rare opportunity to claim for your own the literary field that is richer and broader in French Canada than in any other portion of the globe.—Fiction based on the lives and characters of these quaint and simple people could be made more picturesque than any I know of.—Think about this and study the 'Habitan' in his native simplicity."

And again to the same:

"You ought to jot down in your note-book the words and phrases of patois that you hear—the speech of the common people. You should certainly make notes of what you see and hear—the traditions that are cropping out among the older people."

As is well known, Joel Chandler Harris's earliest work was on newspapers in Forsyth, Macon, and Savannah, Georgia, and later in Atlanta. From the first he had a keen sense of the responsibility of a journalist. Writing in 1876 in "The Lounger," a column which he conducted on a weekly paper, he devoted several paragraphs to this topic:

"An editor must have a purpose," he insisted. "He must have in view some object beyond the mere expression of an opinion or the publication of a newspaper. The purpose may be moral, social or political, but it must be well defined and pursued constantly. I shudder when I think of the opportunities the editors in Georgia are allowing to slip by. It grieves me to see them harping steadily on the same old prejudices and moving in the worn ruts of a period that was soul-destroying in its narrowness. There has never been a time when an editor with a purpose could accomplish more for his state and his country than just at present. What a legacy for one's conscience to know that one had been instrumental in mowing down the old prejudices that rattle in the wind like weeds."

Upon the founding in 1907 of *The Uncle Remus Magazine* of which he was editor until his death more than a year later, he had an opportunity of which he took full advantage to express himself along the lines quoted above, and the flower of his editorial work and his essays is to be found in the first thirteen issues of this periodical. What might he not have accomplished for his section now so terribly in need of intelligent and honest leadership, had he lived to carry on through his magazine, which had a large and high-class cir-

culation in the South and Middle West, his
editorial crusade for straight thinking and toler-
ance!

In writing to one of his daughters, he once
said as he commended her for progress in her
classes, "I knew from your letter that you had
fallen under some sweet yet powerful influence,
and you had begun to learn how to think and
how to think *right* which is the end and aim of all
education."

This note of "right thinking" is the *"leit-motif"*
of the editorial announcement which ushered in
the new magazine and in which the editor states
that *The Uncle Remus Magazine* will be a Southern magazine by reason of its environment, but
that all its motives and policies will be "broader
than any section and higher than any partisan-
ship." And after paying tribute to that beneficent provincialism which is the occasion for the
variation of types, the editor stated that "those
who will be in charge of the magazine will have
nothing to do with the provinciality so prevalent
in the North, East, South and West which stands
for ignorance and blind prejudice, that represents narrow views and an unhappy congestion
of ideas;" on the contrary, he added, "the magazine will hold itself against party politics and
prejudices, and will refuse to mistake opinions
for principles or to be limited by the prolific **and**
offensive suggestions of sectionalism."

His most persistent efforts as an editorial writer were directed toward disseminating a type of "neighbor-knowledge," as he aptly termed it, which would dissipate sectional jealousy and mis-understanding, as well as religious and racial intolerance. He longed for the people of his own state and section to conquer their sensitiveness to rational censure and to cultivate the tonic habit of self-criticism, for he realized that until their intelligence reached this level no real prog-ress was possible.

In discussing the handicaps which threaten the courageous and sincere writer in the South, he referred more than once to the foolish idolatry of tradition which prevents many Southern people from facing their section's problems squarely, and which leads them to treat their own writers with harshness when the latter dare state facts as they are. On this point he wrote in *The Uncle Remus Magazine* some time in 1907:

"Our romantic tendencies always threaten to run away with us; and we are dreadfully senti-mental on the slightest provocation, permitting our local politics to interfere with what should be art. What great writers we might have in our Southern states if only we could make our tra-ditions and our environments contributory to our fictive art! But it seems there are things we cannot deal with familiarly—things we cannot touch with our finger-tips without drawing a bloodblister on the unseemly forehead of politics, and when our writers take their pens in hand, and begin to set forth in fiction the things with which they are familiar, and about which they have first-hand knowledge, they unconsciously feel that they are under some sort of pledge not to offend the abnormal sensitiveness of their neighbors. This has been so and is so, and we shall never have any great novel from the South until our writers shake off this Old Man of the Sea, and free themselves from the imaginary pressure under which they labor. Those who would understand what I mean will do well to recall the hot criticism and social ostracism occasioned by George W. Cable's extraordinary studies of creole life in New Orleans. Mr. Cable was as sensitive in regard to his art as his critics were in respect to the life he depicted, and he straightway betook himself to alien skies, bag and baggage."

Again, in *The Uncle Remus Magazine*, under the pseudonym of "Anne Macfarland," who is supposed to be an American woman living in England, he says of a bigoted attitude toward another of our most accomplished writers:

"Occasionally I have an opportunity to read some of our home-made magazines that are saved for me by an English publisher. Those that I happened to select, not long ago, were either angrily or humorously in pursuit of Henry James. Two of his offenses stand clearly out: he had been unfortunate enough to criticize the oral use of the English tongue by the young women of our republic, and he had been bold enough to invent a diction of his own for the presentation of his ideas. Where his diction is not made a subject of ridicule, he is derided because he has 'expatriated' himself, because he does not choose to live in New York or Boston. All this is supremely silly and is pretty certain to disgust people of real taste and feeling no matter where they live."

Of course, the author of "Free Joe" and "Blue Dave" had no patience with manifestations of injustice toward the negro. More than that, he had active sympathy with efforts such as that of Booker Washington and other educators for the enlightenment and special training of the race. His views on this subject were expressed in detail in a series of three articles published in *The Saturday Evening Post* of January 2nd and 30th and February 27th, 1904. I wish I had space to quote at length from these articles but since this is impossible I will give a significant paragraph, one bearing on the subject of "higher education" for the negro:

"It has been said that the negro race is not yet in a position to be benefited by higher education. This is true, of course, but it by no means follows that all the work that has been done in that direction has been thrown away. In this, as in many things, much has been done that a little may avail. It would be unjust to the negro race to make comparisons, but it is fair to say that a good deal of the higher education that is bestowed on the white race is worse than thrown away, if we are to view the matter from a purely practical and commercial point of view. You hear little of those who believe in education purely for its own sake. They have been crowded to the wall, and whatever their hopes and beliefs may be, they seem very small. Nevertheless, and in spite of the spirit of commercialism which is making our politics more hideous than ever, there will always be some people somewhere, white or black, to profit by what is called a liberal education, and the solace they will be able to receive therefrom, and the service they will be able to perform for their kind will more than repay the leakage and losses, to use a familiar commercial expression."

In an issue of *The Uncle Remus Magazine*, Mr. Billy Saunders, the rural Georgian selected as his political mouthpiece, says of the harsh judgment often meted out to the negro race on account of the criminal acts of a few:

"Let a bow-legged nigger come along an' do his devilment, an' right straight we lay the responsibility on the whole nigger race. We never stop to consider that these debauched nigger criminals don't stand for the whole colored race an' we constantly want to fergit what never should be forgot—that whar thar's one of these sons of Satan, thar's ten thousand decent, industrious, well-behaved niggers. I've hern folks say thet all niggers look alike to them, but they don't all look alike ter me, an' they never will, not whilst my eyesight's good. Thar's jest as much difference betwixt niggers as thar is betwixt white folks, en a heap mo', ef you know the races right well."

On the subject of lynching, this downright old fellow expresses his opinion in picturesque terms to a group of Atlanta newspaper men after the unfortunate "race riot" in that city:

"You fellows up here seem to have a keen appetite for immigration, but how kin you git good men to come up here whar crime calls for the mob an' the rope? Oh, no! you got to git over the idea that mob law helps anything or anybody. It hurts everything, fust an' last. An' I say you got to grab yourself by the roof of your trousers and rise to thet point whar you can see for yourself that the rights of the community, state or county—the rights to peace, law and order—are a heap more important than the rights of individuals."

Old Billy follows up this thrust by some wise words on the need of the people for honest leadership:

"The people have been told by the one-horse politicians so many times that they are always right, an' they have been flattered and flunkeyed

to by the fellows that want office for sech a long
time that they've begun to believe that their
voice is the voice of the Almighty, an' they are
reely some punkins. But the plain facts is that
there never was a time that they couldn't be
fooled and fooled bad, by the cheapest politician
that ever toted a flask of whiskey on a stumpin'
expedition. The people are alright when they
can git honest men to lead 'em, but when, as
today, the perfessional politician is a-straddle of
the lead mule the people are mighty apt fer to be
wrong."

Considering the unorthodoxy of this racy line
of talk, it is not surprising that the editor of *The
Uncle Remus Magazine* received several anonymous letters, the sense of which was that "old Billy
Saunders" was coarse and not a bit funny. But
this did not halt the old fellow in his frankness
and unsqueamishness—indeed, he even went so
far as to attack business greed and the evils of
monopolies, and to suggest to parents a sensible
way of bringing up boys and girls—ticklish
subjects for an old bachelor from the collards
patch!

On dealing with young people, he often expressed himself in his own person, and his views,
as can easily be imagined, were colored by his
genuine sympathy with youth. He had no hard
and fast rules with his own children and guided
them through love and a sense of humor and

an appeal to their self-respect. A hint of his method is to be found in the following passage in a letter to his son when a schoolboy in Canada:

"I am sending you a little book about Emerson. It is time you were beginning to take a little interest in thoughtful things, and you will find in this book some remarks on style that may be profitable to you. Another thing—when I make a remark or a suggestion, don't take it too seriously. All I can do is to give you some of the results of my experience. I am much more interested in seeing you grow up strong-bodied and clean-minded than I am in your career.— I should like to see you with a will strong enough to resist all forms of temptation. Your career will then take care of itself. And yet I shouldn't like to see you puritanical and narrow-minded. I want you to grow up to be a wholesome, hearty, liberal-minded individual."

This warning against being "narrow-minded and puritanical" is frequently repeated in his letters to his boys and his gentle sermons are always keyed to a sympathy with life and its possibilities and its joys. His text was never "Thou shalt not," but rather, "May you be all that Providence meant you to be, in honesty, in happiness, and in helpfulness to others."

Said he in one of his last editorials for *The Uncle Remus Magazine:*

"It is not old age I have been thinking about all this time, but youth—the youth that follows youth somewhat like a circus procession—the youth that is one of the whims of the Farmer.[1] He has many peculiarities, but this is what he calls a *whim*, in spite of the fact that it seems to be an outgrowth of his temperament."

And as he approached the end of his life, an end so premature, so unexpected, he became more and more enamored of the spectacle of youth, its enthusiasm, its unsullied faith, its confidence in life. His thoughts often dwelt on the little souls that had gone on to that "country next-door to the world," his own little children and ours, who were to live in eternal youth beyond our vision. Two very fine editorials, "Little Children of Snap-Bean Farm" and "Santa Claus and the Fairies," and a poem of mystical beauty, "It is Good to Grow Old," embodied his feelings and thoughts about the young of this world and the other.

The author of "Uncle Remus" reflected the religious convictions of his family and friends but had little interest in dogma. In his editorial "The Shakespeare of Modern Business" he wrote: "The discrepancies between the religion that is now affected and that taught in the New Testament are large enough to engulf the whole modern

[1] Frequently in his editorials he called himself "The Farmer".

world," a conviction identical with one recently elaborated upon by a distinguished New York preacher on his enforced retirement from a pulpit which he had filled for many years. He developed this theme further, in saying:

"The truth is a simple and commonplace thing and seems hardly worth the trouble of repeating. That is why the preachers sometimes drift into the habit of sensationalism. They know well from experience that to preach the simple truth as it is found in Scripture would be to drive their congregations elsewhere; and if the truth were to prevail in any large way, our whole social structure would come tumbling down."

He added with almost Anatolean irony:

"To be sure, it is not an important structure at its best, but it admirably represents the spirit of the times. It is said that some rich men really pay preachers to pervert the truth so that they may sleep more comfortably in their pews; and that, on the other hand, not a few of the preachers practise what is called economy in theology in order to satisfy those who pay their salaries. Our old friend Satan has been the beneficiary of so many unmoral compromises that he must be strutting around with increased dignity in his dingy domains."

It is easy for one who has followed the course of "the Farmer's" thought in his fiction and essays to see that the spiritual quality of most

importance to him was that of loving-kindness
or charity. One of the benign and lovable old
men in "Sister Jane," in giving counsel to his
young protégé, William Wornum, says of this
generous virtue:

"Charity! Why William, what does Paul say?
Look it up in the Bible! Why, take charity
out'n religion an' what in the name of common
sense would be left? Nothin' but the dry peelin's.
It'd be like takin' corn out'n the shuck. Shucks'll
maybe do for steers an' dry cattle—but you give
shucks to creeturs what's got any sense an' they'll
snort at 'em an' walk away from the trough."

With increasing years the great Southerner
became more and more the mystic, sure of his
intimate relationships with the universe and its
unseen forces, closely in touch with all created
things—a brother to the wind, a neighbor to the
trees, a friend to the essential soul in man. Said
he, "Man is not our only friend and neighbor.
All things about us are capable of inviting neighborliness and dispensing it to those of us who are
wise enough to take advantage of the hospitality
that is constantly offered. . . . The whole rush
and movement of Nature in her vigorous and
insistent moods, belong to neighborliness in the
most significant and satisfactory sense."

And in one of his last editorials he wrote:

"We are mysteriously bound, indeed, not only
to the living but to the dead, and to all who have

ever lived; and no matter how we may conduct ourselves, no matter what whims we may display, no matter what absurd antics we may cut up before high heaven, we know that we are merely reproducing what has been produced before; we are only living, on a little higher or a little lower scale, a life that has preceded us. Only the spirit is different, only the soul is original when we dare give it full play."

It is sometimes argued that a highly developed critical faculty attains its dimensions only at a cost of a decay or stunting of what are popularly called "human qualities." This is obviously not true of the well balanced nature, for in it is demonstrated the fact that the intellect is as much a gift of God as the soul. I have tried to show in the foregoing that Joel Chandler Harris's clear, shrewd intelligence enabled him to penetrate the shams, the injustices and the intolerances of the life of which he was a part, and that, in spite of his almost morbid modesty, he had the courage at all times to raise his voice against social and political vices. On the other hand, his readers long ago sensed for themselves the tenderness and compassion of his nature toward weak and suffering humanity. It was his love of people, in spite of their folly and limitations, which led him to say in all earnestness shortly before his death, "I would not want to live if I had no faith in my fellow-men."

This confidence in man's innate tendency to reach upward, when combined with clear-headedness, courage and a sense of responsibility, makes inevitably toward moral leadership, and these were the fundamental if not generally recognized qualities of Joel Chandler Harris.

BOOKER T. WASHINGTON

Creator of a Race Epoch

BY

MONROE N. WORK

BOOKER T. WASHINGTON

Booker T. Washington was a pioneer in the real sense of the word. When he came to Alabama in 1881, to establish Tuskegee Institute, he could have made this school similar to other Normal schools. Instead of taking, however, a ready-made curriculum and putting it into the school, he first made a study of the conditions of the people and then endeavored to adapt the courses in the school to meet the needs of these conditions. Here was an indication of that originality and intuitive insight which characterized his whole life and work. What the conditions were among the Negroes in Alabama and how he went about getting first-hand knowledge of them is told in his own words, as follows:

"I reached Tuskegee, as I have said, early in June, 1881. The first month I spent in finding accommodations for the school, and in travelling through Alabama, examining into the actual life of the people, especially in the country districts, and in getting the school advertised among the class of people that I wanted to attend it. The most of my travelling was done over the country roads, with a mule and a cart or a mule and a buggy wagon for conveyance. I ate and slept with the people in their little cabins. I saw their farms, their schools, their churches."

One of the things which he learned soon after beginning his work at Tuskegee was the very important part that public opinion on the race question had to do with a Negro school. He states, "One of the first questions that I had to answer for myself after beginning my work at Tuskegee was how I was to deal with public opinion on the race question. I had not gone very far in my work before I found myself trying to formulate clear and definite answers to some very fundamental questions. The questions came to me in this way: The colored people wanted to know why I proposed to teach their children to work. They said that they and their parents had been compelled to work for two hundred and fifty years, and now they wanted their children to go to school, so that they might be free and live like white folks—without working. Some of the Southern white people, on the contrary, were opposed to any kind of education for Negroes. Others inquired whether I was merely going to train preachers and teachers or whether I proposed to furnish them with trained servants. Some of the people in the North understood that I proposed to train the Negro to be a mere 'hewer of wood and drawer of water,' and feared that my school would make no effort to prepare him to take his place in the community as a man and a citizen."

Booker T. Washington might have sought to avoid the issues raised and gone along the line of least resistance.   Instead he decided to adopt a policy of honesty and frankness. "After thinking the matter all out," he states, "I made up my mind definitely on one or two fundamental points. I determined: First, that I should at all times be perfectly frank and honest in dealing with each of the three classes of people that I have mentioned. Second, that I should not depend upon any short cuts or expedients merely for the sake of gaining temporary popularity or advantage, whether for the time being such action brought me popularity or the reverse. With these two points clear before me as my creed, I began to go forward."

It was in this spirit that Booker T. Washington sought to deal with the race problem as it confronted him in the founding of Tuskegee Institute. Thus it came to pass, that he built a school around a problem, or, putting it another way, he made the education of the Negro a method of dealing with the race problem.

An important phase of the race problem was the question whether the Negroes as a group would acquire sufficient economic efficiency to take their place in the nation as free men. This depended in a large measure upon their attitude toward labor, working with the hands. The attitude of the Negroes toward labor in the Reconstruction Period and immediately after was a heritage from slavery days. They considered labor as the work of slaves; further, when you were really and truly free, you did not have to labor. They brought Biblical support for this attitude by pointing out that a part of the curse that God put upon Adam was that man should labor, should be compelled to earn his bread by the sweat of his brow. A story is told of an old colored man who spent considerable time trying to convince Mr. Washington that, from the experience of Adam in the Garden of Eden, it was a sin to work.

Booker T. Washington set out to change this attitude about labor by teaching the dignity of labor. The substance of this doctrine was that they should dignify and glorify common labor, and should put brains and skill into the common occupations of life.

In one of his Sunday evening talks to students and teachers at Tuskegee, he said:

"People, as a rule, take two views of the object of work. One is the old view; the other is the new view. The old view considers work as something placed in the world as a curse, as a punishment for people; and then in connection with that same idea, people formerly regarded work as being something placed here for the purpose of enabling one to earn a living.

"Both of these views are short sighted. There is scarcely a pig in Alabama that is not able to earn its living. A human being who is only able to do this, is not very much beyond the pig. The new view changes this view of labor. Persons have learned by experience to look upon work as a privilege, as something that is placed here for the highest benefit of human beings.

"It does not apply to any special race, to any special nation, or to any special period of time. You will find that when races or nations get to the point of looking upon labor as a privilege, they are making real progress. The successful nations or races, all that have really made a place in life, you will find always without exception, that they are the races or nations that have learned how to work, to labor; they have learned that it is a privilege to work. They have learned that labor constitutes a part of the highest service of any race or nation."

Along with the idea of the dignity of labor, Booker T. Washington also advocated that education should be made common, that is not only should it be placed within reach of all; but it should also have as subject matter the common things of life. When this is done, then education ceases to be exclusive, ceases to be for gentle folk only. A vital connection is established between education and labor. The result is that a new point of view is reached with respect to labor.

In another of his Sunday evening talks at Tuskegee Institute, he urged that:

"We must make education common—common as the grass, as the sunshine, make it so common that everybody will feel that education is not a vague far off something, dwelling in the midst of the supernatural.

"All that I am trying to urge upon you is to connect your school work, your educational work, with the actual life of the community, because the very minute that people can understand that everything inside the schoolroom has a vital connection with their own life, it will have an interest for every family, every child, every individual in that community, and from that very moment our schools are going to be generously supported in every part of the South. We must make the kind of connection that I have indicated between school life and rural community life."

Booker T. Washington's preaching concerning the dignity of labor, making education common, becoming efficient, he put into practice by developing at Tuskegee Institute a system of education which dignified labor, made education common and increased the economic efficiency of the Negro. The development of Tuskegee Institute met the objections of the Negroes with regard to labor in that they saw it in a new light. This development met the objections of the North in that the people there saw that the Negro was being trained to take his place as a man and a citizen. It helped to remove the opposition in the South to Negro education, for by connecting education with every-day life, it was made practical and a benefit not only to the Negro but also to the South.

The next advance in Booker T. Washington's policy of making education a method of dealing with the race problem was to endeavor to show to white and black alike that only through coöperation, working together, could they prosper. They would rise or fall together. The white man could not rise and at the same time keep the Negro down. This was formulated in that famous expression, "You cannot keep a man down in a ditch unless you remain down there with him." How the black and white might live and work together was set forth in the now famous Atlanta address in which was advocated the doctrine that white and black in the South could live side by side and "be one in all things essential to mutual progress."

The importance of this address was that it formulated a program for whites and blacks to work each for their own advantage, for their mutual interests and for the prosperity of the South. This was not a new doctrine or the advocacy of something that had not been tried. Whites and blacks had been living side by side; they had been working and making progress. What Booker T. Washington did was to point out that what was needed was not some untried method of dealing with the race problem; but rather the developing and extending of the things which were already being done.

The Atlanta address was on the one hand a plea to the Negro to let down his bucket where he was into the opportunities of the South. It was urged that no place in the world afforded greater opportunities for his progress than the place in which he was living. The Atlanta address was also a plea for the Negroes to have more faith in the white people among whom they were living. "To those of my race who depend on bettering their condition in a foreign land and who underestimate the importance of cultivating friendly relations with the Southern white man, who is their next-door neighbor, I would say: 'Cast down your bucket where you are.' Cast it down in making friends in every manly way with the people with whom you are surrounded." To the white people it was a plea to have more faith in the Negro. To them Washington said:

"To those of the white race who look to the incoming of those of foreign birth and strange tongue and habits for the prosperity of the South, were I permitted I would repeat what I say to my own race: 'Cast down your bucket where you are.' Cast it down among the eight millions of Negroes whose habits you know, whose fidelity and love you have tested in days when to have proved treacherous meant the ruin of your firesides. Cast down your buckets among these people who have, without strikes and labor wars, tilled your fields, cleared your forests, builded your railroads and cities, and brought forth treasures from the bowels of the earth, and helped make possible this magnificent representation of the progress of the South. Casting down your bucket among my people, helping and encouraging them as you are doing on these grounds, and to education of head, hand, and heart, you will find that they will buy your surplus land, make blossom the waste places in your fields, and run your factories. While doing this, you can be sure in the future, as in the past, that you and your families will be surrounded by the most patient, faithful, law-abiding and unresentful people that the world has seen. As we have proved our loyalty to you in the past, in nursing your children, watching by the sick-bed of your mothers and fathers and often following them with tear-dimmed eyes to their graves, so in the future in our humble way, we shall stand by you with a devotion that no foreigner can approach, ready to lay down our lives, if need be, in defense of yours, interlacing our industrial, commercial, civil, and religious life with yours in a way that shall make the interests of both races one. In all things that are purely social, we can be as separate as the fingers, yet one as the hand, in all things essential to mutual progress."

Booker T. Washington spent the twenty years, the period from the delivery of the Atlanta address, 1895, to his death in 1915, in endeavoring on the one hand to meet the needs of the Negroes, and on the other hand in working for the bettering of race relations. In endeavoring to meet the needs of the Negroes, he developed Tuskegee Institute into an institution whose original methods of instruction have profoundly influenced present-day vocational training. At the same time, the school, incidentally, became famous throughout the world.

Another way in which he endeavored to meet the needs of the Negroes was by establishing and promoting agencies for reaching and aiding the masses outside or beyond the direct influence of the school room. This was an attempt to

educate the people on the soil. When Booker
T. Washington died, Tuskegee Institute
was carrying on more than twenty-five different
extension activities designed to improve the general welfare of the Negroes in agriculture, in education, in home life, in health, in religion, and in
business. One of the most important of these
agencies is the Annual Tuskegee Negro Conference, which each year brings to the school large
numbers of farmers from every part of the South
to learn about better methods of farming and how
to improve not only the farm, but likewise the
farm home, the school, and the church. Out of the
Annual Tuskegee Negro Conference has grown a
number of other agencies for improving farming
conditions, such as the Agricultural Demonstration Work, the Movable School, and the Short
Course in Agriculture.

For the purpose of stimulating and improving
the Negroes' business opportunities, there was
established in 1900 the National Negro Business
League. Among the important results of the
establishing of this organization for business improvement were, that the Negro business men of
the country became acquainted with each other,
and from this contact they got information and
inspiration; other persons were influenced to go
into business; negro business men were brought
prominently before the general public; local business leagues were organized in all sections of the

country. The League, through its annual meetings and in other ways, has continued to stimulate and promote race enterprises. It is today, one of the most important factors in Negro business progress.

Booker T. Washington early saw that in order for the Negro to make permanent progress, it was necessary for him to improve his health conditions. Almost from the founding of Tuskegee Institute, it was made a health center. A hospital and nurse training school were early made a part of the institution. Later a fifty thousand dollar hospital was erected, which became a health center for the entire Lower South. The National Negro Health Week was established as a direct effort to spread information concerning health improvement among the Negroes throughout the country. In sending out the first appeal for the observance of National Negro Health Week, Mr. Washington said, "Without health and until we reduce the high death rate, it will be impossible for us to have a permanent success in business, in property getting, in acquiring education, or to show other evidences of progress. Without health and long life, all else fails. We must reduce our high death rate, dethrone disease, enthrone health and long life. We may differ on other subjects, but there is no room for difference here. Let us make a strong, long united pull together."

One of Booker T. Washington's most extended
and continued efforts for improving the conditions of the colored people on the soil was by
assisting in the improving of the rural schools of
the South, by directing Negro farm communities,
in the building of school houses, in the lengthen-
ing of school terms and in the securing of competent teachers. He was mainly instrumental in
securing for this purpose the Anna T. Jeanes
Fund of one million dollars to be applied toward
the maintenance and assistance of elementary
schools for Negroes in the South. He also secured
from Mr. Julius Rosenwald money to assist in
erecting rural school houses for Negroes in the
South.   An important feature of the work for
school improvement was that it afforded a means
of improving race relations in that the cooperation of whites and Negroes is secured in improving school conditions.   This is strikingly illustrated through what has been accomplished by
the Jeanes Foundation and the Rosenwald School
House Building Fund.

In 1913, the work of the Negro Rural School
Fund of the Jeanes Foundation was carried on in
121 counties of the South; these counties that
year contributed toward the salaries of the
Jeanes supervising teachers $3,402. In 1924, the
work of the Jeanes Foundation was carried on
in 289 counties, and the counties contributed

from the public funds toward the paying of the Jeanes supervising teachers $144,423.

The condition of the Rosenwald School House Building project was that the people in the community where a school house was to be erected should secure from the public funds, or raise among themselves, an amount equivalent to or larger than that given by Mr. Rosenwald. In the ten years, 1914 to 1924, since the Rosenwald School House Building campaign was begun, 2,500 Rosenwald schools have been erected at a total cost of $10,255,851. Of this amount $2,307,593 was contributed by Negroes, $503,098 by whites, $5,548,683 by public school authorities, and $1,866,477 by Mr. Rosenwald.

In addition to what was done through school improvement work to bring about better race relations, Booker T. Washington worked more directly towards this end. He spent a great deal of time in interpreting the Negro to the South and the South to the Negro, all for the purpose that better race relations throughout the South might obtain. This was done through articles in newspapers and magazines, through addresses on special occasions, but more especially through what came to be known as his "educational tours."

One of his notable articles with reference to improving the conditions under which Negroes lived was published in the Century Magazine, November, 1912, under the title, "Is the Negro

Having a Fair Chance?" After citing some of the advantages under which the Negro lived, it was pointed out that there was still a question as to whether he was having a fair chance. There was the difficulty experienced in obtaining a square deal at all times. There was, for example, the dissatisfaction because of unequal accommodations in railroad travel, the lack of a square deal in education, the evils of the convict system, and the crime of lynching.

In this article Booker T. Washington took occasion to advocate the ballot for the intelligent Negro. Concerning this he said: "In my opinion it is a fatal mistake to teach the young black man and the young white man that the dominance of the white race in the South rests upon any other basis than absolute justice to the weaker man. It is a mistake to cultivate in the mind of any individual or group of individuals the feeling and belief that their happiness rests upon the misery of some one else, or that their intelligence is measured by the ignorance of some one else; or their wealth by the poverty of some one else. I do not advocate that the Negro make politics or the holding of office an important thing in his life. I do urge, in the interest of fair play for everybody, that a Negro who prepares himself in property, in intelligence, and in character to cast a ballot, and desires to do so, should have the opportunity."

Booker T. Washington's educational tours consisted in spending a week or ten days in traveling over a particular state and making a number of speeches each day to crowds of whites and Negroes. The first of these educational tours was made in 1905 in the states of Arkansas and Oklahoma. From that time until his death, similar tours were made in Delaware, parts of Virginia and West Virginia, in North Carolina, South Carolina, Georgia, Florida, Tennessee, Mississippi, Louisiana, and Texas. "My purpose," he said, "in making these educational campaigns was not merely to see the conditions of the masses of my own people; but to ascertain also the actual relations existing between the races, and to say a word, if possible, that would bring about more helpful relations between white men and black men in the communities which I visited." It was a general custom wherever he spoke on his educational tours to have one or more addresses from the leading white persons present. This was a very important step in race relations; for up to this time such a thing had not been done to any great extent anywhere in the South, that is, white and black meeting together and talking face to face to each other. Concerning this, he said: "One of the advantages of the educational campaigns is that they have given an opportunity to Southern men to stand up in public and say what was deep down in their hearts with regard to the Negroes, to express a feeling toward the Negro that represents another and higher side of Southern character and one which, as a result of sectional feelings and political controversies, has been too long hidden from the world."

That Booker T. Washington had a fundamental program is indicated by its successful continuation since his death. The lines of work which he laid down are being carried on and further developed. Tuskegee Institute, on the one hand, under his successor, Robert R. Moton, is continuing to assist in meeting the needs of the Negroes and in promoting "good will" between the races. On the other hand the Inter-racial Coöperation movement is continuing, through organized efforts, to carry on the work of improving race relations. Through this agency coöperation between the races is being promoted in a large way, and efforts are being put forth to assist in giving the Negro a fair chance, a square deal.

MADELINE McDOWELL BRECKINRIDGE
Herald of Community Service

BY

SOPHONISBA P. BRECKINRIDGE

MADELINE McDOWELL BRECKINRIDGE

It is perhaps well to state briefly the few biographical facts that must be kept in mind in any attempt at a review of the slightly more than two decades of the public service of Madeline McDowell Breckinridge, a pioneer in social interpretation and social work in the South.

She was born May 20, 1872, in Franklin County, Kentucky, the youngest but one in a family of seven children, two other daughters and four sons. The youngest child, a boy, died at the age of four; the other children all survive her. When she was ten, her father, Major Henry Clay McDowell, named for the "Great Commoner" but related to him only by having married his granddaughter, Anne Clay, bought "Ashland," the home of Henry Clay, lying just outside of Lexington and owned by his descendants until 1866, when it passed into the ownership of the State A. and M. College, the Land-Grant College of Kentucky. There she lived until her marriage, and there she and her husband had, as it were, a second home; for her mother lived there until February of 1917, an aged and beloved aunt until December of 1918, and a devoted sister with her family still lives there.

She had a peculiar sense of identification with Kentucky, with Kentucky's past as well as with Kentucky's present. In fact, a "sense of the past," to use Henry James's phrase, was in all her feeling for the present and in all her aspiration for the future. To understand this, one has only briefly to recall the part her ancestors played in the earlier Kentucky of heroic deeds.

Her father's great-grandfather, Samuel McDowell, was associated with the pioneer days of privation and exposure, and with the struggle to organize an independent state government as well as with efforts to secure greater safety and comfort in living conditions. Born in Pennsylvania of Calvinist immigrant parents, he moved in 1784 from Virginia, where his parents had made their later home, to Kentucky; was one of the three justices presiding over the first district court in Kentucky, and later was one of those presiding over the first county court, and presided over a series of nine conventions whose protests led to the recognition of Kentucky as a separate state. Her grandfather, also Samuel McDowell, fought in the Indian wars and was first United States marshall for Kentucky in 1792. His younger brother, Ephraim, her great-uncle, was a pioneer in the field of surgery, and performed in 1809, under conditions of great personal peril, the first operation in ovariotomy. Her grandfather, William Adair McDowell, another beloved and distinguished physician, published in 1842 a treatise on the "Curability of Pulmonary Consumption in All Its Stages;" and on one of the highways entering the city stands a memorial to the civic contributions of her father, to whose teaching and companionship she was greatly indebted.

In her mother's veins ran the blood of the Harts, whose name is associated with the dream of western empire registered in the Transylvania enterprise, and of Henry Clay, whose home at Ashland was from the earliest years of the nineteenth century a place of almost pious pilgrimage to visitors from other countries as well as to citizens of the United States. Lafayette, Harriet Martineau, Webster, Thackeray, Olmsted, are a few of the names on the roll of distinguished persons who sought and enjoyed its hospitality. Here she learned to know and to enjoy nature and formed friendships with those of every age and of all economic levels. With all who cherished beauty and desired to convert principle into conduct, she was at home. She loved books, too, and from these varied sources, she enriched her own thinking and living. She was very active until about 1893 when she became the victim of a malady that limited her physical activity. In appearance, she was tall and slender, with great dark eyes, soft abundant brown hair, and an "orator's mouth" very like that made familiar in the pictures of Henry Clay. By nature she was merry and full of gaiety, with quick response to every appeal for help or for sympathy, and with a voice of rare quality, wide range, and irresistible charm. Perhaps her dominating characteristic, however, was fearlessness, the fearlessness that stands undaunted before suffering and death not only, but likewise before life and its problem.

Her public service began at a moment of great community excitement. One afternoon in February of 1899, a brutal murder was committed on the streets of Lexington by a member of a criminal political gang who had enjoyed the protection of the law-enforcing agencies of the city. No steps were taken by the authorities either to hold the murderer, or, after he escaped, to re-apprehend him. She had already become active in the club organization of the city and the women at this crisis attempted to develop a plan by which the murderer's arrest might be secured and a beginning made in the creation of respect for the law and the courts. She was chairman of the committee framing the resolutions at that time and it is not surprising that, as her personal interest in public undertakings had such an initiation, during the following twenty-one years of her unceasing public effort she was likewise unceasing in her emphasis on the relation of orderly processes to sound progress, so that she was never deceived into accepting the statutory enactment divorced from honest enforcement and efficient administration.

She was, in this first instance, not satisfied with effort looking to apprehension and punishment. A study of the neighborhood from which the murderer and his associates came brought home to her the fact that it was a neighborhood of "mean streets," poor houses, unskilled and underpaid labor, and, above all, of neglected childhood, without facilities for schooling or for play. Into that neighborhood she went bearing some of the gifts so greatly needed, and today there stands above the homes, overlooking the slopes of the precipitous streets, a noble school building, serving not only to instruct the children but to minister to the neighborhood needs as well. A gymnasium, a swimming pool, a playground, a laundry and a community kitchen, make it a place in which "all sorts and conditions of men" find aid and comfort and skilled service. It does not bear her name although the Board of Education asked that it might; for, at her request, it was named the Abraham Lincoln School.

It is not true, of course, that she accomplished this alone or all at once. The agency through which the task was achieved was the Civic League, an organization formed for the temporary and emergency work connected with the murder, which functions yet, nobly and competently in behalf of the children of Lexington, and especially of the part of Lexington known as "Irishtown," from which the gang had come. The methods used by the league are of especial interest only in one respect. She had great confidence in public service. She was accustomed to the idea of public office being nobly held. But she was not unaware of the ignoble aspects of public life and she believed in the largest possible coöperation between public and private agencies.

Her plan for this coöperation was a somewhat uncommon plan. She did not resort to the usual device of initiating by private effort a piece of experimental work and after a reasonable period of fair success in a limited field persuading the public authorities to take over the undertaking. This plan has many elements of weakness, namely, that those who have been concerned to initiate are generally absorbed in again initiating and are therefore not at hand to lend swift aid when the plan is subjected to the new tests of universality and of continuity. For public undertakings by their very nature must, in theory at least, be universal and continuous, and these tests are almost never applied to private undertaking. Her plan was for coöperation in the sense that private resources, pecuniary and human, were placed at the disposal of the public authority under conditions agreed upon by the two. That is, the Abraham Lincoln School is one of the public schools of Lexington under the Board of Education. It is, however, much more, because of the constant coöperative association of the Civic League in its work.

It should perhaps have been pointed out that her work, during the period intervening between this first public undertaking and the Thanksgiving Day of 1920 when the curtain fell on the drama of her effort, fell naturally into four sections, closely related but distinguishable the one from the other. The first of these was the effort in behalf of the Lincoln School enterprise and its corollary, the development of legislative protection for children whose needs were like those of the Lincoln School children. This included drafting and pushing Juvenile Court, Child Labor, and Compulsory Attendance laws for cities of the class to which Lexington belonged, if similar laws could not be obtained for all the children of Kentucky; it meant campaigning throughout the whole state in behalf of these measures, and laboring to secure the election of public officials who would enact and enforce and administer these laws in the spirit in which they were urged upon the people of the state. It meant persuading the ablest and most devoted persons to stand for election, and working generously but frankly and persistently with those who were placed in these offices that were of much significance to her.

A second cause to which she gave in unstinted measure was that of sound family welfare work. She was not a college graduate. Her father, undoubtedly with her full consent and agreement, had thought that the loss of four years from the community she loved and meant to serve would mean in loosened ties and slackened interest greater loss than could be compensated for by the severe discipline of the college course. She was for a time a student in what is now Kentucky University (the A. and M. College it was then called), and went for two happy years to Farmington, Connecticut. One of the friends of that association was a volunteer worker for the New York Charity Organization Society. With her friend she attended lectures on family care, and became greatly interested in the principles of the charity organization movement, indeed thoroughly converted to those principles. She was ever after that an adherent of the most devout and unflinching sort to the doctrine of sound case-work. And when, in February, 1900, at a time of great unemployment and distress, the mayor asked the charitable ladies of the city to take over the distribution of the city's outdoor relief, she was prepared to coöperate in developing a plan which would offer every applicant individual and, to an extent, skilled service. In this plan there was again an attempt at coöperation between public authorities and private

agencies of the kind she believed in and was willing to undertake.

As the situation developed, the Associated
Charities took on likeness to the usual private society subsidized from public funds. It has never
been quite that, however; it was rather a private
organization delegated to do certain tasks for the
city and county, for which the administrative
authorities of those jurisdictions provided the
resources. The task, the responsibility, and the
authority were definite and the methods to be
applied likewise agreed upon, namely those of
sound and thorough case-work. There could be
no doubt on any of these points. This meant continuous education and re-education of the city
and county officials and her associates as well.
And sometimes this was a difficult and thankless task. One year, for example, an organization,
not dominated by these principles of case-work,
an organization that neither investigated before
attempting to give treatment nor gave frank and
full accounts of its stewardship, asked to be and
was included by the city among the agencies
authorized to perform certain functions in the
field of public relief. This she would not endure,
and, single-handed, as a tax-payer, she sought
and obtained an injunction against the payment
by the city to the recalcitrant organization.

The third field of conspicuous effort on her
part was in the field of public health, and grew

especially out of her own experience in suffering
and lessened physical power. Shortly after her
return from school she had been the victim of an
accident which seemed at first to be followed by
no serious consequences but resulted later in
serious physical limitation that necessitated her
spending several winters in the south or west
and held its threatening hand always before her.
The winter of 1903-4, she spent in a sanatorium
in Denver and while there she informed herself
concerning the waste, economic, social, and above
all human, connected with the inadequate provision for the early care and treatment of victims
of tuberculosis. She had been interested in the
medical aspects of the problem through her study
of her grandfather's writings, and she now became deeply concerned for its social and govern-
mental aspects as well. On her return from
Denver, then, she associated with herself those
members of the community most concerned for
public health matters and most intelligent with
reference to the care and treatment of this particular disease. Out of this organization grew an
association now known as the Public Health Nursing Association and an organization concerned
for the establishment of a county sanatorium.
There also resulted from these activities the passage of a bill creating a State Tuberculosis Commission, of which she was a member for four
years, when she resigned because of partisan po-

litical interference on the part of the governor. The commission has since that time been placed as a permanent division of the work of the State Department of Health, the principles for which she fought have been recognized in connection with the establishment of state sanatoria, and the Blue Grass Sanatorium, like the Lincoln School, stands and, above all, serves by way of cure and treatment for the sick of the city and county in which she lived in perpetual reminder of the devotion she felt to principles enunciated over a half-century before by her grandfather and worked out by her for the most helpless members of the community.

A fourth effort to which she devoted her time and strength was the "Votes for Women" movement or the "Suffrage Cause," as it used to be called. It was inevitable that she should be an ardent suffragist, witnessing as she daily witnessed, the neglect of causes for which women have tacitly assumed and acknowledged responsibility, even when not demanding the power with which competently to deal with that responsibility. She could obtain the assistance of the most politically influential men; but they, while they found it not too difficult to put through measures socially important or socially disastrous in which large groups of men or special interests were concerned, found themselves strangely impotent when they undertook to push the measures for

which the women asked. It was not that the
public mind had not been prepared; the mind of
only half the public, to speak roughly and yet
with essential regard for the fact, felt concerned.
From the time at which the census figures of
1900, published only several years later, made
known the pitiful condition of Kentucky's population in the matter of illiteracy (Kentucky was
fourth from the bottom of the list of commonwealths in order of the literacy of their population), she had expended great energy as member
or chairman of one of the divisions of the State
Federation of Women's Clubs whose responsibility it was to secure legislation with reference to
the school system and to arouse interest in that
system. She therefore read the school laws of
other states, studied the problems of school finance, and familiarized herself with the devices
invented in other commonwealths for dealing
with the rural as well as with the city school
system. She consulted the most skilled drafts-
men, and attempted to secure for Kentucky the
laws that seemed most likely to meet the needs
of Kentucky's people. She learned, however, by
sad and repeated experience, what theory told
her in advance, that political effort without political power is apt to be fruitless. And so, even-
tually, she turned largely, though never exclusively, to the suffrage fight.

She became in 1912 president of the Kentucky Equal Rights Association, was called on to write for the monumental History of Woman's Suffrage the account of the movement in Kentucky after 1900, and she succeeded in obtaining from the Kentucky legislature unprecedented action on the opening day of the session of 1920 ratifying the Nineteenth Amendment to the United States Constitution, so that Kentucky was one of the early states to go on record in favor of this grant of power to the women of the state.[1]

In connection with her suffrage work it is perhaps necessary to make only two points here. First, she had a great sense of the importance of the work in the states. She had learned by her legislative work in the most remote and isolated portions of Kentucky the value, when decisions were being framed at the capital, of public opinion "back in the district." She was therefore never sympathetic with a policy that devoted exclusive attention to Washington. She had, however, a thoroughly national mind. She believed the political status of women in any state to be of concern to the people in all the states, and she therefore, from conviction, fostered and supported in every way the effort to secure the

---

[1] Attention may be called to the fact that Kentucky early recognized the principles of women's votes. In 1838, widows with children in school were granted the right to vote on school questions.

amendment to the constitution of the United States. The other point is that the suffrage was always to her chiefly an instrument with which was to be carved out a nobler commonwealth. She was therefore never willing to sterilize the movement for the sake of obtaining the vote at a little earlier date. She would make no compromises for the sake of success in this movement that would jeopardize those other movements for which she was so concerned. She had at times to withdraw from executive positions, or to declare herself in ways that were dangerously frank, lest she be later apparently committed to concessions she would never consent to make. She served on the Executive Board of the National American Woman Suffrage Association during the year 1914, that is from December 1913 until the spring of 1915, and resigned lest there be some such question for her position as has been referred to. She received national recognition in various ways. She addressed the National Association, in this field, just as she appeared before the National Conference of Social Work, or the National Playground Association or served on the National Board of the General Federation of Women's Clubs (1910-1912), and she traveled from one end of the country to the other, when she was able and she felt that she could serve the cause.

There is in fact no way in which one can portray the effort she put forth for these causes that seemed to her so important. Reference has been made to the fact that from about 1893 her health was precarious. Yet any estimate of the travel she did, the speeches she made, the correspondence she carried on, the organizations she perfected, would appear such an exaggeration as to seem only incredible. The call would take her suddenly into distant "campaign states" where for considerable periods of time she would speak under the most untoward conditions, possibly several times a day at different places, traveling from place to place in any available conveyance.

When the federal amendment was ratified, she turned eagerly to the plans for the League of Women Voters and to the aspirations of women of other lands, and in the summer of 1920 she went as a delegate to the meeting of the International Suffrage Alliance at Geneva.

It has been said that she had a national mind. She had the international mind as well. She was not a Pacifist, although a devoted admirer of Miss Addams to whom she always turned for help and never without the most generous and sympathetic response. But her father had been an officer in the Union army and, while her mother's brothers had divided on the great issues of the Civil war, her childhood was not overwhelmed with the memories of a "Lost Cause" nor had her soul been eaten into by the bitter sense of the futility of all war. But she longed for peace and she believed in law and in the rule of good-will. She therefore became an ardent advocate of the League of Nations and to that end supported the democratic presidential ticket in 1920. Her last public effort was devoted to two weeks of incredibly arduous campaigning in Missouri in behalf of that program.

In the preceding paragraphs little has been said of her private life. And yet it should be made clear that all these activities to which so much space has been given were those of a woman whose chief business was that of a devoted wife, daughter, and friend. To those relationships one can only refer. She never forgot, she never neglected. The simple tribute of the poet,

> "She doth little kindnesses,
> That most leave undone or despise.
> For naught that sets one's heart at ease
> Or giveth happiness or peace
> Is low-esteemed in her eyes,"

might well have been written of her. She has been called a great citizen, and she was that. But a review of her twenty-one years of rich service takes the mind back to the ardor of the early Charity Organizationists for the Volunteer. And she was an example of what the great volunteer could be. It was not only that she was not paid;

sometimes, in fact, she took payment for her speeches. She did not want to underbid, and she was always begging and "raising" money for some of her causes. But she was under no compulsion other than that of a great idea of her responsibility and of her opportunity. Moreover, the peculiar values of the service of the volunteer are (1) that they represent the normal instead of the pathological; and (2) there is no measure or standard by which they can be judged except the principles of sound work. The professional worker must inevitably have in mind a day's work, that is an item in a week's work, that makes up a part of a year's total. The volunteer need do no tomorrow's work until today's work is done as it should be done. There may be, therefore, characteristic of the volunteer's product, a freshness and a brilliancy and, often, a completeness, not always found in the work of the most skilful professional, and sadly rare under the conditions of underpreparation, over-work and under-pay so often characteristic of the conditions under which social work is carried on.

These features characterized her work in all its aspects. No labor was too great, no effort too arduous, no detail too insignificant. She was humble-minded in her willingness to sit at the feet of any from whom she hoped for a clew. No instrument was too insignificant to experiment with. She felt no self-consciousness, she sought no publicity for herself, she shrank from no publicity that might serve her cause. She lived in the face of a great purpose and, with all the effort, there was a great serenity as there always was a great simplicity and a swift gaiety.

It is always difficult to write of her, for one is conscious of the skill and delicacy with which she would have been able to do the task. She had a great love for the word whether written or spoken, and delighted in skilful selection and fine discrimination. On the other hand, the rudest hand cannot greatly mar the beauty of so great and free a service. And it is always an enriching experience to recall that in the associations and memories and institutions and activities that abide, her life is worked into the very warp and woof of her state, her section, and her nation.

EDWARD KIDDER GRAHAM

Apostle of Culture and Democracy

BY

ROBERT D. W. CONNOR

EDWARD KIDDER GRAHAM

Edward Kidder Graham was the product of his time and environment. The time was the last two decades of the nineteenth century, the environment an old-fashioned Southern town in an old-fashioned Southern state. It was a period of transition wherein the people of the South were trying desperately to adjust themselves to new political, social, and economic conditions.

The first step in this adjustment was taken when at Appomattox the South surrendered its "sectional belief in leisure and caste to the national ideal of Democracy and Work," and entered upon its "titanic task of complete material reconstruction." The problems which the Southern people had to solve were to democratize their political institutions without sacrificing their ideals, "to industrialize their society and to modernize their spirit without commercializing their souls."

There were those who feared that the adjustment could not be made except at the sacrifice, without compensating gains, of much if not all that had been fine and beautiful in the culture of the Old South, but Graham was not of their number. What it meant and how it could best be accomplished nobody understood more clearly

than he. He pinned his faith to "the belief that
Democracy and Work constitute a truly cultural
principle," quite as real as that of leisure and
caste. However he had his own definition of culture which to him was not a matter of knowledge
and taste but a mode of life. "Culture," he
wrote, "is not a knowledge of the creeds of religion, art, science, or literature. . . . it is not a
study of perfection through 'coming to know'; it
is the development of the spirit through work—
it is *achievement touched by fine feeling.*"

Since "culture is the complete art of life,"
"Democracy is its main active manifestation."
Therefore, as President Edwin A. Alderman says:

"The word culture was, next to democracy, oftenest upon
his lips, and I am convinced that the innermost urging
of his life was to comprehend completely these two great
postulates and to relate them to each other so that there
would issue in the contacts of common life about him
a vitalized culture and a humanized democracy. . . .
[Democracy] was not to him a mere political or phil-
osophical slogan. It was a religion, a spirit, a principle
of life and service. His orderly mind had long since
established the kinship and interdependence between
education and democracy, and his flaming spirit had
admonished him that they must be made to know each
other better and serve each other better."

By establishing this complete accord between
education and democracy, Graham believed the
South could make its adjustments without sacrificing its ideals or commercializing its soul, and

the instrument he chose for this task was the state university. "The state university," he said, "is the instrument of democracy for realizing all of the high and healthful aspirations of the state." His election as president of the University of North Carolina in 1914 placed in his hands perhaps the best instrument then in the South for such a purpose. President Alderman states the case in the following passage:

"There could not have been found a better platform or sounding board from which to conduct his operations and preach his policy of education and life than the University of North Carolina. It was an ancient State University, saturated with a practical democratic atmosphere, capable of sustained enthusiasms, of steadfast aims, institutional unselfishness, and buoyant hope. A serene good fortune lifted him to the presidency of this institution, which he loved as if it were made of flesh and blood, in the prime of life and at the moment when a war of liberation from outworn tyrannies burst upon the world, releasing all men's energies and heightening and purifying all men's spirits. With a vision clear and far-reaching, a patience that was boundless, a sympathy that knew no limits, a steely energy that relaxed only to spring into greater strength, he adventured upon the task of tying together in one whole fabric the needs of the people and the resources of learning. The methods he used were as diverse and varied as the problem he sought to solve. Like Cardinal Newman he flung himself again and again at the task of defining and analyzing the functions of universities and democracies. . . . But he was too wise to neglect the pragmatical and practical or to slight the technical and scholarly aspects of the problem. And so the University grew in scientific authority as well as in social approach."

Graham was indeed fortunate in finding such an instrument ready fashioned for his hand, and was generous but just in acknowledging and evaluating the contributions made to it by his predecessors. His own task was to use this instrument as an aid to the South in passing from a culture of leisure and caste to a culture of democracy and work. To make clear the use he made of it we must first state, as nearly as possible in his own words, his conception of the function of the modern state university in the life of the modern democratic state. He thought of the state university not as a thing apart from present-day democracy, but as an organism functioning in every vital phase of its life. As such, therefore, there is no concern of the modern state that is not also the immediate concern of the state university. Its function is not only to search for truth, but also to set truth to work in the world of living men and things, to liberate the spirit of men from the tyranny of time and place, not by running away from the world, but by mastering it. The democratic state can not realize its highest and most healthful aspirations until all the forces in it that make for a fuller, richer, and freer life, in education and in business, in science and in religion, in industry and in politics, are thus liberated and guided by "a

confident and competent leadership" inspired by
a passion for truth. This leadership he conceived
it to be the function of the state university to
furnish, not in the spirit of selfish ambition, but
in the spirit of sympathetic and unselfish service.

This conception of the function of the state
university in general, Graham sought to make
concrete in the University of North Carolina in
particular. Different universities, he declared,
can show different reasons for their existence and
for being what they are, for all have come into
being in response to certain needs of their time
and place, and though all may be inspired by
essentially the same purpose, the search for
truth, the manifestations of this purpose must
from the very nature of such institutions be as
diverse as are the diverse needs of their different
constituencies. The State of North Carolina is
the constituency of the University of North Carolina; therefore, its needs and aspirations are
that University's chief concern. Nobody recognized more clearly than he that truth is not a
local matter, and that the true standards of life
are not local but world standards, but what he
did see more clearly than most of his contemporaries is that the universal truth which the
University of North Carolina should seek first
of all, could not become vitalized for North Carolina except through service in interpreting and
solving North Carolina's problems. "What the

University sees," he said, "is, that no matter how disinterested and universal the truth it seeks, North Carolina is the immediate medium of its interpretation." He therefore saw the University's fundamental problem as a question of the intensity, purity, and radiating power of its inner spirit and its creative and curative power in the particular civilization it serves. Since it is to its creative and constructive power as an institution of liberal culture that its peculiar value in the life of North Carolina is due, its chief function is to put all its forces of culture and knowledge into the active service of the State.

This conception of the state university's function assumes, of course, that the spirit and purpose of its organized life shall be in harmony with the spirit and purpose of modern democracy. In Graham's efforts to re-fashion the University whose fortunes he directed for this new service three features stand out with peculiar distinctness. They are the evolution which took place under his leadership in the spirit of the inner life of the students; the introduction of the principle of democracy in university administration through faculty coöperation; and the bringing of the University into closer and more sympathetic contact with the life of the democratic state through its extension service.

Students were encouraged to adopt standards of college life and conduct that aimed at "the development of a normal, healthy, responsible, and, at the same time, happy manhood." President Graham sought to aid them in reaching this goal not by relaxing the bonds of discipline, nor by lowering the standards of conduct and scholarship, but by making the one an expression of self-control and self-direction, and by showing how the other might be put to work in the service of humanity. The simple principle was adopted that students were expected to attend to all duties. Thus the center of administrative control of student conduct passed from faculty to student-body, negative policies of compulsion gave way to affirmative policies of self-direction, and fearsome proddings from without yielded to the promptings of the spirit from within.

There were those who saw the dangers of such a policy and hesitated to follow President Graham's leadership. He, too, saw the dangers, but beyond the dangers he saw with clearer vision a goal well worth striving for. "Every big human policy," he said, "is dangerous, for the reason that it is a human and not a mechanical policy." The test of such a policy is whether it works, and that depends upon the nature of the material it works with. President Graham's whole conception of the function of the state university as applied to his own particular University was founded in faith in the nature of the material he worked with, and the results justified his faith.

After a fair trial of his policies, he was able to report that the necessity for punitive discipline for deliberate misconduct had practically disappeared and penalties for failure to meet university duties were no longer necessary. The difference was a difference in attitudes. Performance of college duties became not a matter of rules but of personal obligation, while self-government passed the self-conscious stage and became as truly a part of the normal life of the college community as it is of the life of any democratic community in the larger world.

President Graham's faith in the spirit of democracy was also revealed in his relations with his university colleagues. His attitude towards those he worked with was well described by his secretary in the following passage:

"It was not the fact of his leadership, but the way in which he led, that won my respect, later my admiration, and finally my love. He never sought to dominate or overawe, or subdue anyone, but to make every man his own master. He wanted no servants, no subordinates about him. He never told a man to do this or that; if he had to tell a man what to do he had no need for him. He wanted about him men with a purpose, with a work, and a plan of their own. And it was in this broad, free way that he was making of the University of North Carolina a distinctive institution. The men associated with him felt, not that they were working for him, but that he was giving to them a medium and opportunity for doing in the biggest way the thing they wanted to do. Around him men felt free."

Around him men *were* free! He might, as one of his colleagues says, "reveal to them new and vital lines for their own work," but he never used compulsion upon them to accept his views. On the other hand, he freely and sincerely sought their advice and coöperation, but he desired it only when freely and sincerely given. He not only invited and encouraged full and frank discussion by the faculty of university affairs and policies, but took the faculty into partnership by placing in its hands the selection of certain important policy-making committees which had previously been appointed by the president. To say that there were critics among his colleagues who did not fully accept his leadership, is simply to say that the University faculty was composed of human beings; nevertheless, as a group, the faculty welcomed the innovation, willingly accepted its share of administrative responsibility, and entered heartily into the spirit of the new régime.

Indeed, President Graham's success in his larger policies was chiefly due to his ability to win support for them both within and without immediate university circles. Behind the translation of his ideas into realities, and assuring its success, lay the active and healthy coöperation which his leadership called forth from students and faculty, from alumni and trustees, and from the whole people. Their almost universal spirit of coöperation is indeed the best evidence of the attitude of the State toward his work and of its confidence in his genius for high and splendid leadership.

Internal organization, whether of student-body or of faculty, was simply President Graham's means to a greater end, the interpretation of scholarship in terms of service. There were scholars whose first impulse was to protest against the indignity done to scholarship and men of affairs who could scarcely conceal their contempt for the practical value of such service as scholarship had to offer. But Graham, with his conceptions of culture and democracy, saw no indignity to scholarship in making it serviceable, and he was convinced that democracy in all its various social and economic phases had much to gain from contact with the spirit and methods of scholarship. He insisted, on the one hand, that scholars should "emphasize the fact that research and classical culture rightly interpreted are as deeply and completely service as any vocational service," and he urged them to "consider their service too precious to be confined in cloisters and sufficiently robust to inhabit the walks of men;" on the other hand, he sought to impress upon men of affairs the idea that though the state university "regards any practical need as an opportunity for service," its still larger service is in so perfecting the relations of work to life that any

worthy industry may be made "a liberal voca-
tion in saving the man and all his higher faculties,
not from business but through business." Thus
his philosophy of culture and work dignified scholarship by putting it to work in the service of
mankind, and strengthened and liberalized the
forces of constructive democracy by impregnat-
ing them with a passion for truth and the methods
and spirit of truth-seeking.

In this process he thought the state university
has a double part to perform. Its "main and
special" function is to teach, not because it thus
confers certain personal benefits upon the taught,
but "because the most direct and deepest way of
reaching the sources of state life is through the
organized instruction of the youth of the State."
The state university, therefore, necessarily con-
centrates its strength on its own campus, but it
must understand that its campus is not its only
field of service, nor the instruction of a group of
selected youth its only mission. Its campus is
the State, its mission, service to all the people.

On this basis the University of North Carolina under his leadership built up a distinct type
of extension work. The origin and development
of this extension service illustrates the sort of
faculty coöperation that President Graham encouraged. He did not originate extension service
at the University; he found it in operation when
he became president. What he did was to make

the idea his own, to expand, liberalize and vital-
ize it, to interpret it to the State, and to make it
effective. The University of North Carolina does
not conceive of extension as an appendage to its
"main and chief function," but rather as an or-
ganic part of it. It has no specific extension
faculty; its extension work consists in actually
"extending" to non-resident students, its regular
courses through its regular staff. Through its
normal machinery of lectures, laboratories, libraries, research, and publications, it undertakes
to place all its various agencies of scholarship at
the service of the State and to apply universal
truths and world standards to the State's peculiar problems of business, agriculture, commerce, education, health, and religion. This service the University interprets, in the words of
President Graham, "not as thinly stretching out
its resources to the State boundaries for purposes of protective popularity, nor as carrying
down to those without the castle gates broken
bits of learning; but as the radiating power of a
new passion, carrying in natural circulation the
unified culture of the race to all parts of the body
politic."

The University had long felt that the State
did not live up to its obligations to it; President
Graham taught a different point of view. He
was not concerned with the obligations of the
State to the University, but he was deeply con-

cerned with the obligation of the University to the State. If, on the one hand, he taught the University to think of its chief function as service to all the people, "not as sacrifice, but as life, the normal functioning of life as fruitful and fundamental as the relation between the vine and its branches," on the other hand, he taught the State to see that the problems and the needs of the University of North Carolina are not merely those that are normal in its nature as an institution of learning, but those also that are peculiar in its nature as an institution of the State of North Carolina, and as such they must automatically multiply under the pressure of the ever-quickening, expanding life of that State and its rapidly increasing material strength.

It never occurred to him but that if the University fully met its obligations to the State, the State would respond in kind. He said in his inaugural address:

"What it [the University] asks, and all that it asks, is not for itself, but as the common instrument of all men concerned in advancing the general welfare and the more abundant life of the State. For this reason it confidently asks, in the first place, for the sympathetic understanding and interest of all those who work with a decent and and reasonable regard for the common good, and it asks for such support as will enable it worthily to assist in the solution of the common problem. If it conceives of its task as one that calls for great equipment, it is not because it is blind to certain limitations, but because it sees beyond limitations to latent powers just as actual and far more real; and finally, and beyond all this, because it has sure, supreme, and practical faith in the greatness of the State whose representative it is."

Thus he magnified the place of the University in the life of the democratic state because in doing so he magnified democracy; and the greatness of his vision caught the imagination of the State and awakened it to a realization of its latent powers and possibilities. He asked democracy to think greatly of itself, and the response was immediate and sympathetic; indeed, the people of North Carolina seemed to feel that he had but made articulate ideals that they had long cherished, and when he came to translate those ideals into realities the forces of constructive democracy felt the stirrings of a new and stimulating spirit radiating from the State University.

None of those who were present will ever forget his appearance before the General Assembly in the critical year 1917, when on the battle-front in France the fate of democracy was hanging in the balance, nor the quick response which the General Assembly, and then the whole State, made to his statement of the function, not of the University only, but of education in all its grades and through all its agencies in the life of a democracy. He repeated to the General Assembly

in substance what he had already said in his
report to the Board of Trustees:

"Educationally the decade that follows the war will
be, I believe, the richest and most fruitful in the nation's
history. Here in the South, . . . we need to keep heroically
foremost in our public policy the determination not to
slacken, but rather to quicken our educational activities
during the war. England and France under war burdens
incomparably greater than ours have doubled their
educational budgets. It is clearly the inevitable policy
of wisdom.

"Our handling of our educational affairs in the next few
years will furnish once more a test of our statesmanship
and give once more a clear revelation of what relative
place we give education in the things worth while in
commonwealth building. The necessity of war economies
will show what we value in terms of what we nourish and
of what we sacrifice. . . . No sacrifice is too great to make
for the schools, and no patriotism is more genuinely
productive than the patriotism whose faith in the schools
is so deeply rooted that no public distraction or disaster
is permitted to blight them as the source of all of our
reconstructive power."

The response of the General Assembly to this
appeal took the form not only of liberal increases
in appropriations for education, but also of complete acceptance of President Graham's views,
acknowledgment of the State's new and greater
obligations resulting from them, and the reversal
of a century-old fiscal policy founded on self-
depreciation, narrowness of vision, and timidity,

in favor of a policy founded "on the courage of investment, the courage of leadership, the courage of growth toward greatness."

The attitude of the people toward the State University also underwent a complete change. Formerly regarding it with disfavor as the pampered pet of a privileged few, they came to accept it as in reality the instrument of democracy for realizing all the high and healthful aspirations of the democratic state.

It was inevitable that President Graham's ideas and policies should attract widespread attention especially in the South. It was to the South primarily that he spoke when he defined the "Function of the State University" in his inaugural address. The "next great expansion in national life," he prophesied, would be in the South;

"here will be the focusing point of the world's commerce; the summons that puts the eager and prophetic tone in Southern life today is the consciousness that here under circumstances pregnant with happy destiny men will make once more the experiment of translating prosperity in terms of a great civilization. It is to leadership in this supreme adventure of democratic commonwealth building that the universities of the South are called, and their real achievements depend upon the sure intelligence, sympathy, and power, with which they perform their vital function and make authoritative answer to the compelling question of the people as to what, if anything, in the way of clear guidance they have to offer, or must we look to another?"

Accordingly other Southern state universities watched the development of his policies in North Carolina with interest and skepticism. Like the old University of North Carolina they were fine representatives of what Walter Page called "the aristocratic scheme of education," and like the Southern people generally they were loath to surrender their old ideals. "Socialized universities," serving all the needs of all the people, might do well enough in the new West and Middle West, but in the older South conditions were different! Within more recent years, however, tendencies in the South indicate a change of heart. The culture of democracy and work has everywhere triumphed over the culture of leisure and caste, and educational institutions are feeling a new stimulus. To what extent the work of Graham in North Carolina, ably continued and expanded to cover a larger field by his successor, has contributed to this result, it would be difficult to say, but this much is certain, other Southern universities, after careful surveys and studies of the workings of the North Carolina plan, have accepted the idea in full or with such modifications as are necessary to meet local conditions; and the idea of the "socialized university" and the "state-wide campus" has become a vital force in Southern education. In formulating and working out this idea in the South the pioneer work was done at the University of North Carolina under the leadership of Edward Kidder Graham.